Interpreting Basic Statistics

A Guide and Workbook Based on Excerpts from Journal Articles

Fifth Edition

Zealure C. Holcomb

Pyrczak Publishing
P.O. Box 250430 • Glendale, CA 91225

"Pyrczak Publishing" is an imprint of Fred Pyrczak, Publisher, A California Corporation.

Although the author and publisher have made every effort to ensure the accuracy and completeness of information contained in this book, we assume no responsibility for errors, inaccuracies, omissions, or any inconsistency herein. Any slights of people, places, or organizations are unintentional.

Project Director: Monica Lopez.

Cover design by Robert Kibler and Larry Nichols.

Editorial assistance provided by Cheryl Alcorn, Randall R. Bruce, Karen M. Disner, Brenda Koplin, Jack Petit, Erica Simmons, and Sharon Young.

Printed in the United States of America by Malloy, Inc.

ISBN 1-884585-71-X

Contents

Continued →

*New to this edition

*New to this edition

Continued →

*New to this edition

*New to this edition

Introduction to the Fifth Edition

This book presents brief excerpts from research journals representing a variety of fields, with an emphasis on the social and behavioral sciences. The questions that follow each excerpt allow students to practice interpreting published research results.

The questions require students to apply a variety of skills, including:

1. locating specific information in statistical tables, figures, and discussions of results;

2. performing simple calculations to determine answers to questions not directly answered in the excerpts;

3. discussing the authors' decisions regarding reporting techniques;

4. describing and interpreting major trends revealed by data, including evaluating the authors' interpretations; and

5. evaluating procedures used to collect the data underlying the statistics presented.

Although the excerpts emphasize the "results" sections of the journal articles from which they were drawn, some information about procedures, such as sampling and measurement, is often included in order to put the results in context.

Some Assumptions Underlying the Development of This Book

A major assumption is that students will find materials based on actual research reports inherently more interesting than the hypothetical examples typically presented in research methods and statistics textbooks.

It is also assumed that students will benefit by practicing with materials written by numerous authors. This allows them to see variations in the uses of statistics and in reporting techniques as they are actually used by practicing researchers.

A statistical guide at the beginning of each exercise provides highlights that help in the interpretation of the associated excerpt. The guides are not comprehensive because it is assumed that students using this book are enrolled in statistics and research courses in which theoretical and computational concepts are covered in detail in their textbooks. Thus, the guides should be thought of as reminders of basic points to be considered when attempting the exercises.

Finally, it is assumed that a collection of complete research reports would produce too much material to be integrated into traditional statistics and research methods courses. Instructors of such courses are often pressed for time when covering just the essentials. Hence, this book presents brief excerpts to conserve instructional time.

Cautions When Using This Book

Students should be aware that the exercises are based on excerpts from journal articles. Although the excerpts are in the original authors' own words, many important details presented in the complete articles are omitted in this book for the sake of brevity. Before generalizing from the excerpts, such as in papers written for other classes, students should read the full research articles, which are available in most large academic libraries.

Although answers to the *Factual Questions* are either right or wrong, there may be more than one defensible answer to each of the *Questions for Discussion*. At first, some students are surprised to learn that the interpretation of data is not always straightforward. Yet, it is precisely because of this circumstance that practice is needed in interpreting research results as they actually appear in journals.

Finally, students will discover occasional inconsistencies between what is recommended by their textbook authors and the analysis and reporting techniques employed by the authors of the excerpts. Variations are permitted by journal editors, and the excerpts in this book will help students prepare for reading published research articles that are not always "textbook perfect." When taking tests in class, however, students should follow the recommendations made by their textbook authors and/or their instructors.

About the Fifth Edition

A number of exercises have been updated with new, more timely examples. In addition, some exercises have been added to provide examples of a greater array of statistical examples. The 28 new exercises are identified with asterisks in the Table of Contents.

Acknowledgments

I am grateful to Richard Rasor, professor emeritus of American River College, and Robert Morman and Deborah Oh of California State University, Los Angeles, for the many suggestions they made for improving this book.

Zealure C. Holcomb

Exercise 1   Exposure of Youth to Violence

Percentage: I

Statistical Guide

Percent means "per one hundred." For example, if there are 1,000 residents in a town and 60% are Republicans, then, on the average, 60 out of each 100 are Republicans. To determine the total number of Republicans, multiply 1,000 by 0.60, which yields 600.

To calculate a percentage, divide the part by the whole and multiply by 100. For example, if 8 of the 234 seniors in a high school reported having tried cocaine, then 3.4% reported cocaine use $(8/234 = 0.0342 \times 100 = 3.42 = 3.42\%$ or 3.4%).

Excerpt from the Research Article[1]

Participants consisted of 178 African American youth between the ages of 14 to 19 years… residing within the Detroit metropolitan area. The residency of participants spanned 26 zip codes within the metropolitan area. There were 96 females…and 82 males.

African American youth were recruited from four private high schools and three community youth centers.… It was not possible to survey all classrooms, and therefore 9th- and 11th-grade classrooms were surveyed at each school. This assured that both younger and older adolescents were included in the sample. There were no age or grade restrictions during community center recruitment.

All students in designated classrooms were eligible to participate in the study; however, only those [students] providing signed parental consent forms were administered surveys.… At community centers, youth were informed they could participate in a special activity if they obtained parental permission. Surveys were completed at the youth center. In all cases, participation was voluntary.

Statistics indicate that 85% of the youth had been victims of some type of violence (violence experienced), whereas 91% of adolescents had witnessed some form of violence (violence witnessed).

Table 1
Percentages of Violence Exposure by Gender

Incidence of violence	Victim		Witness	
	Male	Female	Male	Female
Being chased	62	23	80	59
Hit by family	53	55	51	74
Hit by nonfamily	49	32	64	57
Beaten or mugged	19	5	55	32
Sexually assaulted	2	20	10	8
Attacked with a knife	23	9	23	9
Seriously wounded	23	6	53	35
Shot or shot at	42	11	62	38
Shot at/shot someone	20	5	—	—
Witnessed a suicide	—	—	3	3
Witnessed a murder			14	11

[1] Source: Myers, M. A., & Thompson, V. L. S. (2000). The impact of violence exposure on African American youth in context. *Youth & Society, 32,* 253–267. Copyright © 2000 by Sage Publications, Inc. Reprinted with permission.

Questions for Exercise 1

Part A: Factual Questions

1. What percentage of the participants was male?

2. What percentage of the female participants witnessed someone "Being chased"?

3. Did a larger percentage of males *or* a larger percentage of females witness someone being seriously wounded?

4. Expressed as a percentage, what was the difference between males witnessing a suicide and females witnessing a suicide?

5. How many of the females (not percentage) were victims of sexual assault?

6. How many males (not percentage) were seriously wounded (victims)?

7. How many more males than females were the victims of beatings/muggings? (Report your answer to a whole number.)

8. The males were most often the victims of what type of violence (violence experienced)?

9. The females were most often the victims of what type of violence (violence experienced)?

Part B: Questions for Discussion

10. If you sum the percentages under the column labeled "Victim/Male," you get considerably more than 100%. Does this make sense? How is this possible?

11. Would you feel comfortable in generalizing the results reported here to African American youth in public schools in the same metropolitan area? Explain.

12. Do you think that making participation voluntary was a good idea? Could this decision affect the validity of the results?

13. Do you think that when selecting students from the private high schools, selecting only students in the 9th and 11th grades was a good idea? Explain.

14. Do the results of this study surprise you? Why? Why not?

Exercise 2   Hepatitis C and Drug Use

Percentage: II

Statistical Guide

To review percentages, see the statistical guide for Exercise 1.

Excerpt from the Research Article[1]

A representative sample of inmates at intake was obtained…from the Rhode Island Department of Corrections. Serum specimens from mandatory HIV testing were tested for…hepatitis C virus (HCV).

For this analysis, we compared blood test results with injection drug use, which was self-reported to a nurse during intake in response to a question about IV drug use.

Our data comparing laboratory test results and self-reported data are shown in Table 1.

Table 1

Comparison of Presence of HCV Antibody with Self-Reported Injection Drug Use: Rhode Island Prison Study Sample, 1998–2000

	HCV Positive		HCV Negative	
	No.	%	No.	%
Men				
Reported injection drug use				
Yes	306	34.5	61	2.0
No	581	65.5	2983	98.0
Women				
Reported injection drug use				
Yes	110	55.8	13	4.5
No	87	44.2	275	95.5

Questions for Exercise 2

Part A: Factual Questions

1. Of the eight categories of inmates in the table, which category had the largest number of inmates?

2. What is the total number of women who reported injection drug use?

---

[1] Source: Macalino, G. E., Dhawan, D., & Rich, J. D. (2005). A missed opportunity: Hepatitis C screening of prisoners. *American Journal of Public Health*, 95, 1739–1740. Copyright © 2005 by the American Public Health Association. Reprinted with permission.

3. What is the total number of inmates who reported injection drug use?

4. Of the eight categories of inmates in the table, which category had the smallest percentage of inmates?

5. Were there "more men" *or* "more women" in this study?

6. In terms of numbers, more men (306) than women (110) who reported injection drug use were HCV positive. Does the same pattern hold when examining percentages? Explain.

7. What percentage of women who reported injection drug use were HCV negative?

8. What percentage of women who reported no injection drug use were HCV negative?

9. If your answers to Questions 7 and 8 are correct, they should sum to 100%. Do they?

Part B: Questions for Discussion

10. Conclusions can be drawn from Table 1 by examining only the percentages. In your opinion, is the report of the number of cases underlying each percentage helpful? Explain.

11. The researchers use the abbreviation "No." to stand for numbers of cases. If you have a statistics textbook, examine it to see what abbreviation or symbol the textbook author uses and report it here.

12. The researchers determined injection drug use based on self-reports by inmates to a nurse during inmate intake. In your opinion, is this method likely to be perfectly valid? Explain.

Exercise 3   Estimated Substance Use

Percentage and Mean Percentage

Statistical Guide

To review percentages, see the statistical guide for Exercise 1. In this excerpt, students were asked to estimate the percentage of students in their schools who use certain substances. Table 1 shows the means of the percentages for each substance. The *mean* is the most popular average, which is obtained by summing the values for each case and dividing by the number of cases. For instance, if one student estimated that 10% of the students in a school used alcohol in the past week while another student estimated that 20% of the students used it, the mean for the two students would be 15% (10% + 20% = 30%/2 = 15%).

Table 2 in the excerpt shows the actual percentages of students (not means) who self-reported their personal use of the substances.

Excerpt from the Research Article[1]

Subjects for this study were 223 high school students enrolled in health or physical education courses at three separate high schools in the Pacific Northwest.... High School 1 had 72 subjects, High School 2 had 79, and High School 3 contributed 72. The mean age for this sample was 16.1 years. Fifty-six percent of the subjects were juniors, with 17% seniors, 15% freshmen, and 12% sophomores. The sample included 99 females and 124 males.

...it can be concluded that the students in these three high schools had misperceptions of the prevalence of substance use in their respective schools. In general, these students grossly overestimated the percentage of their peers who used [the substances]. In most instances, estimations of the prevalence of a substance use behavior exceeded the percentage of students reporting a particular substance use behavior at a rate of 2–3 times.

Table 1
*Estimations of the Prevalence of Substance Use for Three High Schools**

Substance use behavior	School 1	School 2	School 3
Current marijuana use[a]	50.2%	12.3%	32.5%
Alcohol use in the past week	52.9%	73.3%	39.4%
Binge drinking[b]	35.3%	59.9%	23.3%
Current cigarette smoking[a]	63.9%	56.2%	40.2%

*Mean estimation of percentage of students engaging in a substance use behavior.
[a]Use in the past month.
[b]Five or more drinks of alcohol at one sitting during an average week.

Table 2
Self-Reported Substance Use for Three High Schools

Substance use behavior	School 1	School 2	School 3
Current marijuana use[a]	23.7%	5.1%	14.0%
Alcohol use in the past week	19.5%	35.4%	15.3%
Binge drinking[b]	11.1%	24.0%	9.7%
Current cigarette smoking[a]	27.8%	30.8%	15.3%

[a]Use in the past month.
[b]Five or more drinks of alcohol at one sitting during an average week.

---

[1] Source: Page, R. M., Hammermeister, J., & Roland, M. (2002). Are high school students accurate or clueless in estimating substance use among peers? *Adolescence, 37,* 567–573. Copyright © 2002 by Libra Publishers, Inc. Reprinted with permission.

Questions for Exercise 3

Part A: Factual Questions

1. What was the average age of the students in the sample?

2. Students estimated "Current marijuana use" to be lowest in which school?

3. Students had the lowest self-reported "Current marijuana use" in which school?

4. For School 1, what is the difference between the mean percentage estimate for "Binge drinking" and the self-reported percentage for "Binge drinking"?

5. There were 72 subjects in School 3. Approximately how many of them self-reported "Current cigarette smoking"? (Hint: Convert the percentage to a decimal and multiply.)

6. Approximately how many of the subjects in School 2 self-reported "Alcohol use in the past week"?

7. Were all of the mean percentages for estimated use higher than all the percentages for self-reported use?

8. The results show which of the following general patterns for "Current marijuana use"?
   A. In the schools with higher mean percentage estimates of current marijuana use, there is higher self-reported current marijuana use.
   B. In the schools with higher mean percentage estimates of current marijuana use, there is lower self-reported current marijuana use.

Part B: Questions for Discussion

9. The researchers use the term "subjects" to refer to the respondents in this study. Some style manuals for scholarly writing specify that the term "participants" should be used instead of the term "subjects." Do you know which term is preferred in your field of study? If so, which term is preferred?

10. When researchers ask respondents about sensitive issues such as substance use, they are concerned with the problem of "social desirability." This term refers to the possibility that respondents will answer in a socially desirable direction (e.g., report that they do not use substances) rather than answer honestly. In your opinion, are the data in Table 1 or the data in Table 2 more likely to be influenced by social desirability?

11. The researchers did not include the numbers of cases associated with each percentage in Table 2. Questions 5 and 6 above asked you to calculate two of those numbers. If you had written this report, would you have included the numbers of cases in the table? Why? Why not?

12. If you had planned this study, would you have predicted (i.e., hypothesized) that the mean percentage estimates would be higher than the self-reported percentages? Explain.

Exercise 4   Opiate Addicts Seeking Treatment

Frequency Distribution with Percentages

Statistical Guide

A frequency distribution helps to organize and summarize data. It is a statistical table that shows the number of cases (i.e., frequency of cases that obtained each score). Typically, the scores are listed in order (such as from high to low) in the first column, and the numbers of cases (*n*) are listed in the second column. The percentage of cases associated with each score is often provided.

Excerpt from the Research Article[1]

[Little] is known about heroin and opium use in the Iranian population.... Opium was known to the ancient Persians and has been traditionally used for recreation, for relieving pain, and also for treating mental disorders.

The data were gathered from 306 consecutive addicts who sought treatment at the Shiraz Self-Identified Addicts Center from July to September [in a recent year]. A semistructured interview was carried out with the subjects and one of their first-degree relatives.

The data were gathered from 306 subjects whose mean [a type of average] age was 37.0 years.... Subjects were 97.7% men of whom the majority (73.9%) were married and 24.2% single.

Duration of substance currently used is shown in Table 1. About 36% of the addicts reported that they had been using the current substance for more than a decade. Only 2.3% reported one year or less as the duration of taking the substance.

Table 1 gives the frequency distribution for the longest duration of abstinence. The majority (74.3%) gave a history of abstinence. Only 1.6% reported five years or more as the longest duration of abstinence, while 18.3% indicated one to three months as the longest duration. Overall, 62.1% relapsed before one year of abstinence was completed.

Table 1

Frequency Distribution of Addicts by Duration of Current Opiate Use and Longest Duration of Abstinence Reported (n = 306)

Current use, yr.	*n*	%	Duration of abstinence	*n*	%
< 1	7	2.3	No abstinence	63	20.6
2	19	6.2	< 1 week	18	5.9
3	18	5.9	1 to 4 wk.	28	12.4
4	19	6.2	1 to 3 mo.	56	18.3
5	31	10.1	3 to 6 mo.	44	14.4
6	27	8.8	6 to 12 mo.	34	11.1
7	27	8.8	1 to 3 yr.	29	9.5
8	18	5.9	3 to 5 yr.	6	2.0
9	6	2.0	> 5 yr.	5	1.6
10	24	7.8	No answer	13	4.2
11–15	26	8.4			
16–20	57	18.6			
> 20	27	8.8			

---

[1] Source: Ahmadi, J., & Ghanizadeh, A. (2000). Motivations for use of opiates among addicts seeking treatment in Shiraz. *Psychological Reports, 87,* 1158–1164. Copyright © 2000 by Psychological Reports. Reprinted with permission.

Questions for Exercise 4

Part A: Factual Questions

1. At the time of the study, how many of the subjects had been using opiates for 10 years?

2. At the time of the study, what percentage of the subjects had been using opiates for 10 years?

3. Which current years-of-use category has the largest percentage of subjects?

4. Which duration-of-abstinence category has the largest number of subjects in it?

5. Does the category that you named in Question 4 also have the largest percentage for "Duration of abstinence"?

6. At the time of the study, how many of the addicts had been abstinent for less than one week?

7. Does the last column of percentages in the table sum to 100%?

8. Check the researchers' calculation of one of the percentages by dividing the number who reported no abstinence by the total number in the sample and multiplying by 100. To *two* decimal places, what answer do you get? (Note that the researchers reported the percentages to *one* decimal place.)

9. If you put all the names of the addicts in a hat, mix the names thoroughly, and pull one name out at random, the person you selected would most likely be in which duration-of-abstinence category?

Part B: Questions for Discussion

10. In the table, the researchers list the scores (years) from low (at the top) to high (at the bottom). If you have a textbook that covers this topic, does your textbook author recommend this arrangement? Explain.

11. Most of the scores for current years of use (in the first column) are for one-year periods. Yet some are for larger periods (such as 11–15), and one is for a smaller period (< 1). If you have a textbook that covers this topic, does your textbook author recommend that all of the score intervals be of the same size? Explain.

12. For duration-of-abstinence scores, the score with the lowest percentage is > 5 years. Do you think this indicates that abstaining from opiates over a number of years is very difficult? Explain.

13. Statement: "The percentage in the 16–20 current-years-of-use category is much larger than those in the 9 current-years-of-use category." While this is a correct statement, is there something potentially misleading about it? Explain.

Exercise 5   Supermarket Express Lane Violations

Frequency Distribution without Percentages

Statistical Guide

To review frequency distributions, see the statistical guide for Exercise 4. Note that a basic frequency distribution does not include percentages. However, consumers of research often find it helpful to calculate percentages when interpreting such distributions. To review the calculation of percentages, see the statistical guide for Exercise 1.

Excerpt from the Research Article[1]

[Observations were made] at…an outlet of a supermarket chain located in a suburban community near a large city in the northeastern USA.… It has 11 customer checkout lanes and…one was designated as express for 10 items or less.… The store was open seven days a week, generally 24 hours a day.… Approximately 275 vehicles could be accommodated in the store's parking lot. A total of 68 15-min. observations…were made of the number of items presented by customers using the express lane. Viewings were limited to weekdays: [9 AM to 4 PM]. …data were recorded only if two or more of the other lanes were open, and each had a line of two or more customers.

Recognizing such methodological limitations as the use of a relatively small sample of convenience…, it seems now perhaps only about 7% of shoppers observe the item limit of the express lane.

Table 1
Frequency Distribution of Number of Violations

No. of customers observed exceeding item limit during an observation period	Frequency of occurrence, observation periods
0	5
1	8
2	14
3	17
4	12
5	6
6 or more	6

Questions for Exercise 5

Part A: Factual Questions

1. What is the frequency for three customers observed exceeding the item limit?

---

[1] Source: Trinkaus, J. (2002). Compliance with the item limit of the food supermarket express checkout lane: Another look. *Psychological Reports*, *91*, 1057–1058. Copyright © 2002 by Psychological Reports. Reprinted with permission.

2. In how many observation periods were four customers observed exceeding the item limit?

3. In how many observation periods were *four or more* customers observed exceeding the item limit? (Hint: You must perform addition to obtain the answer.)

4. In what *percentage* of the observation periods were two customers observed exceeding the item limit? (Hint: The total number of observation periods is 68. The table shows that in 14 of the 68 periods, two customers were observed exceeding the limit.)

5. In what *percentage* of the observation periods were three customers observed exceeding the item limit?

6. To statisticians, the values in the first column are "scores." In this particular excerpt, each obser- vation period has a score. Specifically, each observation period has a score that reflects the num- ber of customers who exceeded the limit during the observation period. Given this information, what is the frequency for a score of 5 (i.e., how many times did a score of 5 occur)?

7. What is the frequency for a score of 1?

Part B: Questions for Discussion

8. Table 1 shows that in 6 of the 68 observation periods, 5 customers were observed exceeding the limit. Six out of 68 is equivalent to 8.8% (i.e., $6/68 = 0.088 \times 100 = 8.8\%$). If you were telling another student about this result in a single sentence, which one of the following statements would you make? Explain your choice.

A. Five customers were observed exceeding the limit in 6 of the observation periods.
B. Five customers were observed exceeding the limit in 8.8% of the observation periods.

9. In your opinion, does the size of the supermarket (e.g., has a parking lot that can accommodate 275 vehicles) make a difference in interpreting this study? Might a study using a different size supermarket yield different results? Explain.

10. Is it important for consumers of this research to know that the observations were made on weekdays between 9 AM and 4 PM? Explain.

11. The researcher states that the sample is "small." Do you think that 68 15-minute observation periods is "small"? If yes, how many do you think would be an adequate number?

12. Suppose you obtained funding to conduct a similar study with a larger sample. Which of the following do you think would be a better use of the funds? Explain your choice.

    A. Quadruple the number of observation periods from 68 to 272 at the supermarket.
    B. Quadruple the number of supermarkets from 1 to 4 (maintaining 68 observation periods at each market).

13. If you had written this research report, would you have included percentages in the table? Why? Why not?

Exercise 6   Changes in the Incidence of Asthma
Alternatives to Percentages and Proportions

Statistical Guide

A *percentage* is the *rate per 100*. To review percentages, see the statistical guide for Exercise 1. When a characteristic is very rare, percentages can be awkward to read and interpret. For example, 0.023% of the males in Canada committed suicide in a recent year. This is read as "twenty-three thousandths of one percent," which is quite a mouthful.

To convert a very small percentage to a different rate, use the following multipliers:

If you want to convert a percentage to this rate:	Multiply the percentage by this number: (*Multiplier*)	Example (Canadian male suicide rate)
Per 1,000	10	0.023% × 10 = 0.23 per 1,000
Per 10,000	100	0.023% × 100 = 2.3 per 10,000
Per 100,000	1,000	0.023% × 1,000 = 23 per 100,000
Per 1,000,000	10,000	0.023% × 10,000 = 230 per 1,000,000

To convert some other rate to a percentage, use the following divisors:

If you have one of the following rates and want to convert it to a percentage:	Divide the rate by this number: (*Divisor*)	Example (Canadian male suicide rate)
Per 1,000	10	0.23 per 1,000 becomes: 0.23 ÷ 10 = 0.023%
Per 10,000	100	2.3 per 10,000 becomes: 2.3 ÷ 100 = 0.023%
Per 100,000	1,000	23 per 100,000 becomes: 23 ÷ 1,000 = 0.023%
Per 1,000,000	10,000	230 per 1,000,000 becomes: 230 ÷ 10,000 = 0.023%

Excerpt from the Research Article[1]

Figures 1 and 2 show the trends in the prevalence of asthma and the death rate for asthma.

---

[1] Source of the data: Centers for Disease Control and Prevention. (1995). Asthma—United States, 1982–1992. *MMWR Morbid Mortal Weekly Report*, *43*, 953–955. Figures reproduced from Brown, C. M., Etzel, R. A., & Anderson, H. A. (1997). Asthma: The states' challenge. *Public Health Reports*, *112*, 198–205. Reprinted with permission.

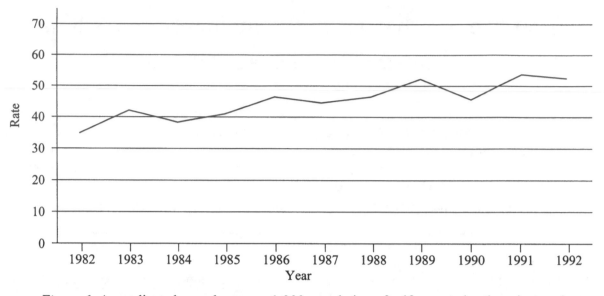

Figure 1. Age-adjusted prevalence per 1,000 population of self-reported asthma in people ages 5–34, by year—United States, 1982–1992.

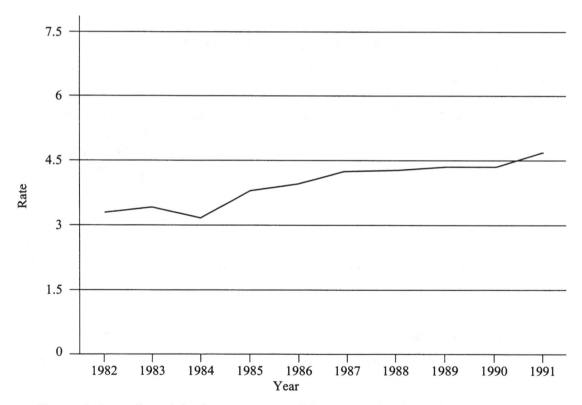

Figure 2. Age-adjusted death rate per one million population for asthma as the underlying cause of death in people ages 5–34 years, by year—United States, 1982–1991.

Questions for Exercise 6

Note: All questions refer to individuals who are 5 to 34 years of age.

Part A: Factual Questions

1. How many people per 1,000 reported having asthma in 1985?

2. What percentage of people in 1985 reported having asthma?

3. In 1991, about 54 in 1,000 reported having asthma. What percentage of the people reported having asthma in 1991?

4. According to Figure 2, about how many people per 1,000,000 died with asthma as the underlying cause in 1991?

5. In 1990, about 4.4 people per 1,000,000 died with asthma as the underlying cause. What is the corresponding percentage?

6. Write your answer to Question 5 in words without using numerals.

7. Suppose 0.15% of people died of another disease in a given year. How many people per 1,000 died of it?

8. For the percentage in Question 7, how many people per 10,000 died of it?

Part B: Questions for Discussion

9. Speculate on why the authors did not use the same rate in both figures.

10. The rate of self-reported asthma dropped from 1991 to 1992 (see Figure 1). Should this be cause for optimism?

11. Describe in your own words the overall trend in the data presented in Figure 2.

Exercise 7   Television Viewing, Books, and Reading
Histogram: I

Statistical Guide

A *histogram* has vertical bars. The scores on a continuous variable are placed on the horizontal axis (i.e., *x*-axis). For example, age is a continuous variable because there are no gaps between the ages of 0 and 1, between the ages of 1 and 2, and so on. The vertical axis (i.e., *y*-axis) shows the frequency, percentage, or rate of occurrence.

An *outlier* is an observation that is far from the other observations. For example, Figure 3 clearly has outliers.

The *mode* in a histogram is the most frequently occurring score. In the figures below, the scores are "Viewing time (hours per week)," "Number of books," and "Amount of reading (times per two weeks)."

Excerpt from the Research Article[1]

Thirty preschool children and their primary caregivers participated. Participants were recruited from Chapel Hill and Durham, North Carolina, public housing communities and Head Start programs.

We assessed the quality of the home environment with items inquiring about the number of children's books in the home, frequency of parent–child joint reading, and parental instruction.

We assessed television viewing with three items, which asked parents to estimate their children's viewing time separately for weekdays, Saturdays, and Sundays; these items were later combined to yield a single index of viewing time per week.

The sample frequencies for the variables reflecting the educational quality of the home environment are displayed in Figures 1–3.

Figure 1. Children's television viewing time.

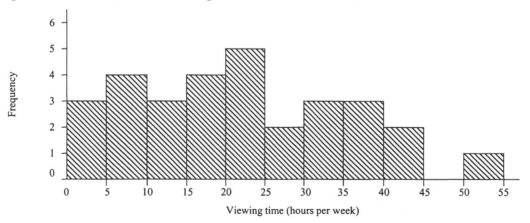

Note: Television viewing time per week for the sample of 30 preschool children from low-income families. Frequency refers to the number of children in each category of viewing time.

---

[1] Source: Clarke, A. T., & Kurtz-Costes, B. (May/June 1997). Television viewing, educational quality of the home environment, and school readiness. *The Journal of Educational Research*, *90*, No. 5, 279–285. Reprinted with permission from the Helen Dwight Reid Educational Foundation. Published by Heldref Publications, Washington, DC 20036-1802. Copyright © 1997.

Figure 2. Children's books in the home.

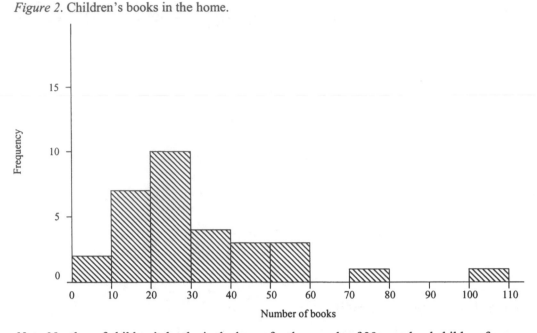

Note: Number of children's books in the home for the sample of 30 preschool children from low-income families. Frequency refers to the number of children in each category of books.

Figure 3. Parent–child reading time.

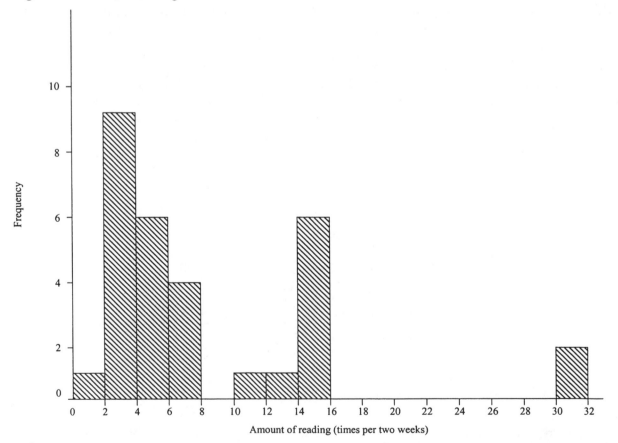

Note: Frequency of parent–child reading interactions in a 2-week period for the sample of 30 preschool children from low-income families. Frequency refers to the number of children in each category of reading interactions.

Questions for Exercise 7

Part A: Factual Questions

1. How many children watched between 40 and 45 hours of television per week?

2. Which number of hours of television viewing (e.g., 0 to 5, 5 to 10, etc.) had the largest number of children?

3. How many children's homes had 20 to 30 books?

4. How many children were engaged in parent–child reading interactions (during the two-week period) from 14 to 16 times?

5. What *percentage* of the children watched television between 20 and 30 hours per week? (If you do not recall how to calculate percentages from frequencies, see the statistical guide for Exercise 1.)

6. In Figure 1, what is the mode? (Hint: In this case, the mode is a range of scores.)

7. In Figure 2, what is the mode?

8. How many children are clearly outliers in Figure 3?

9. Do the bars in any of the histograms form a bell-shaped (i.e., normal) distribution?

10. Some authors of statistics textbooks recommend that the scores be grouped into about 10 to 20 *intervals* for presentation in a histogram. (Note: In Figure 1, the authors have *not* presented a bar for each number of hours but rather for *intervals* of hours, such as 50 to 55.) Do all three histograms in the excerpt conform to the textbook authors' recommendation?

Part B: Questions for Discussion

11. Textbook authors usually recommend that each histogram be given a number and a title, as was done in the histograms in this exercise. Speculate on why the authors make this recommendation.

12. The authors were interested in getting a single, overall estimate of each child's television viewing time per week. To do so, they asked about viewing time separately for weekdays, Saturdays, and Sundays. In your opinion, was it a good idea to ask about television viewing with three questions instead of only one that asks for total viewing time per week? Explain.

Exercise 8   Reading Improvement
Histogram: II

Statistical Guide

See the statistical guide for Exercise 7 for the definition of a *histogram*, *outliers*, and the *mode*. When there are outliers at only one end of a distribution (without outliers on the other end), a distribution is said to be *skewed*. When the outliers are on the right, the distribution is said to have a *positive skew*. When they are on the left, the distribution is said to have a *negative skew*.

Excerpt from the Research Article[1]

The Observation Survey of Early Literacy Achievement (OS; Clay, 2002) is an individually administered assessment tool that is used extensively in the United States and other countries.

The participants in the current study...were 182 first-grade students.... Of these students, 130 had been identified as being at risk for reading difficulty, and 52 were typically developing readers from the same classrooms.

At the beginning and end of first grade, all students ($n = 182$) were individually assessed.... We administered the OS to the participating first graders in September [the pretest] and early May [the posttest] of the same school year. Figure 1 presents the score distributions for the 182 students....

Figure 1. Histograms of Clay's Observation Survey Scales at beginning and end of grade 1 ($n = 182$).

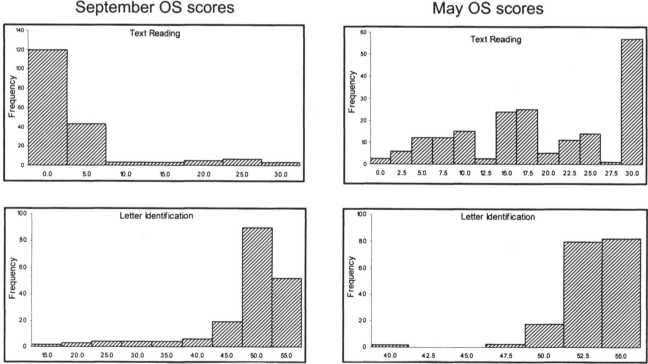

[1] Source: Denton, C. A., Ciancio, D. J., & Fletcher, J. M. (2006). Validity, reliability, and utility of the Observation Survey of Early Literacy Achievement. *Reading Research Quarterly, 41*, 8–34. Copyright © 2006 by the International Reading Association. Reprinted with permission.

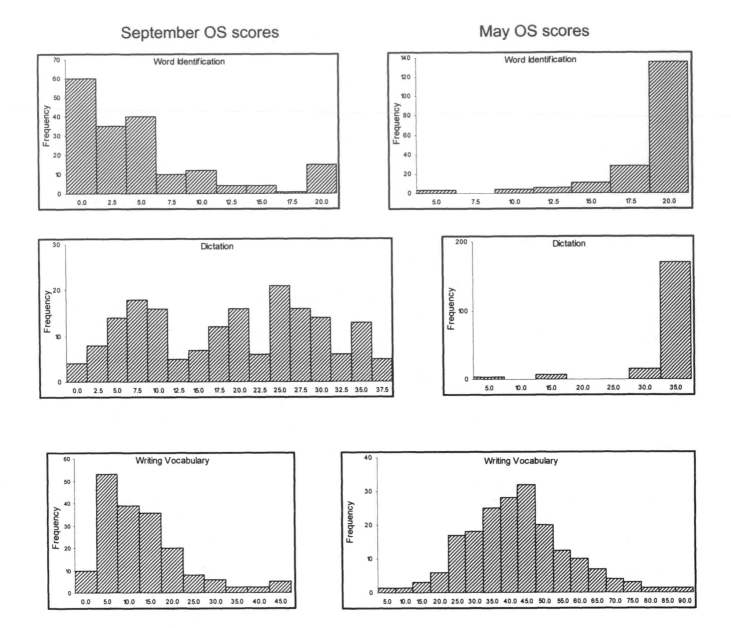

Questions for Exercise 8

Part A: Factual Questions

1. What is the mode for Writing Vocabulary on the pretest?

2. What is the mode for Writing Vocabulary on the posttest?

3. Does the distribution for Word Identification on the pretest have a "positive skew" *or* "negative skew"?

4. Does the distribution for Word Identification on the posttest have a "positive skew" *or* "negative skew"?

5. Which one of the pretests clearly has a negative skew?

6. Which one of the posttests has the least skew (i.e., is most symmetrical)?

7. For which one of the tests is there the least change from pretest to posttest?

8. Which one of the following is more skewed?

   A. Dictation pretest   B. Dictation posttest

9. Which one of the distributions comes closest to having a bell shape (i.e., being a normal curve)?

10. What is the approximate frequency for a score of 50.0 on Letter Identification pretest?

Part B: Questions for Discussion

11. In your opinion, which test is the least useful for measuring reading improvement at the first grade level?

12. Suppose the researchers presented only the average score on each pretest and the average score on each posttest (without presenting histograms). Would this be a better way to present the results?

Exercise 9 Monthly Suicide Rates

Line Graph with Rate per 100,000

Statistical Guide

A line graph can show seasonal changes in behavior. They are especially interesting when they are averaged over a period of several years, which washes out idiosyncratic results that might occur, for example, in one particularly wet winter season.

The line graphs in this exercise show rates per 100,000. To review this concept, see the statistical guide for Exercise 6.

Excerpt from the Research Article[1]

This study attempts to examine the existence of seasonality in suicide rates and the relationship between weather and suicide rate.

Monthly data for suicide...from 1980 to 1994 were obtained from the Hong Kong Census and Statistics Department.

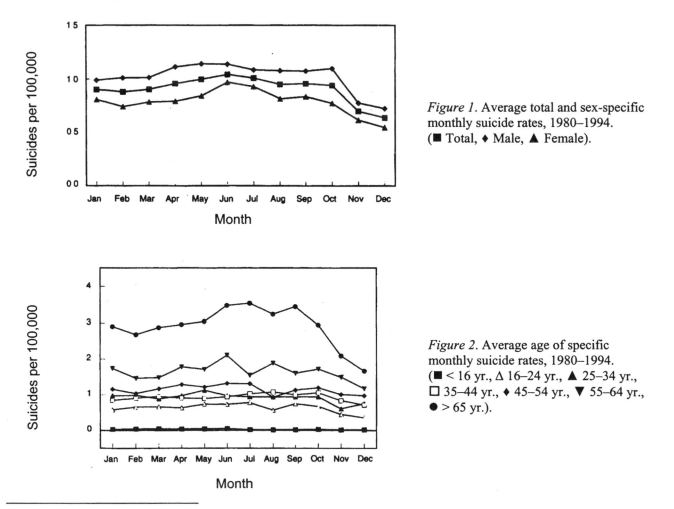

Figure 1. Average total and sex-specific monthly suicide rates, 1980–1994. (■ Total, ♦ Male, ▲ Female).

Figure 2. Average age of specific monthly suicide rates, 1980–1994. (■ < 16 yr., Δ 16–24 yr., ▲ 25–34 yr., □ 35–44 yr., ♦ 45–54 yr., ▼ 55–64 yr., ● > 65 yr.).

[1] Source: Yan, Y. Y. (2000). Geophysical variables and behavior: LXXXXIX. The influence of weather on suicide in Hong Kong. *Perceptual and Motor Skills*, *91*, 571–577. Copyright © 2000 by Perceptual and Motor Skills. Reprinted with permission.

Questions for Exercise 9

Part A: Factual Questions

1. Is the average total suicide rate in January greater than *or* less than 1 in 100,000?

2. Are "males" *or* "females" consistently above the average total across all months?

3. Examine the average suicide rate for males in January in Figure 1. If these data applied to a city with 500,000 males, about *how many* should you expect to commit suicide in January?

4. Examine the average suicide rate for males in January in Figure 1. If these data applied to a city with 1,000,000 males, about *how many* should you expect to commit suicide in January?

5. You should expect what *percentage* of males in Hong Kong to commit suicide in January? (See the statistical guide for Exercise 6 if you do not know how to calculate the answer.)

6. Which age group consistently had the highest suicide rate across the months?

7. For people under 16 years of age in Hong Kong, what *percentage* should you expect to commit suicide in December?

8. Examine the average suicide rate for those older than 65 in April. If these data applied to a city with 700,000 people older than 65, about *how many* of them should you expect to commit suicide?

Part B: Questions for Discussion

9. The data in the figures are for a 15-year period. In your opinion, is this a sufficiently long period to identify reliable trends? Is it much better than examining only one year? Explain.

10. Do you consider any of the trends striking or noteworthy? Explain.

11. The data in the figures could have been presented in a table. Part of such a table is shown imme-diately below. Do you prefer to have the data presented in a line graph or in a table? Explain.

Table for Question 11
Average Suicide Rates Per 100,000[1]

Month	Men	Women	Total
January	1.0	0.8	0.9
February	1.1	0.7	0.8
March	1.1	0.8	0.9
and so on.			

[1] Values are rough approximations from Figure 1.

12. The title of the research article from which these data are drawn refers to "the influence of weather on suicide." In your opinion, do these data strongly support the hypothesis that weather influences suicide rates? Could there be other seasonal explanations? Explain.

Exercise 10 Norms for a Spelling Test
Cumulative Percentage and Percentile Rank

Statistical Guide

A cumulative percentage indicates the percentage of examinees that scored at and below a given score. A cumulative percentage is also known as a percentile rank. For example, if 40 percent of a group had scores equal to or lower than an examinee's score, then that examinee has a percentile rank of 40. Note that percentile ranks are usually rounded to whole numbers when reported to examinees.

Test makers often try out a test with a large group of examinees (known as the norm group) and then build a table such as the one in the excerpt (known as a norms table). Those who subsequently take the test can convert their raw score (number right) to a percentile rank using the table.

Excerpt from the Research Article[1]

This test is composed of 76 words with one or more letters missing. A short line indicates where the letter(s) should be inserted (e.g., exper__ment). Words were selected from lists of the words most frequently misspelled by college students. Brief hints are provided in ambiguous or potentially difficult situations (e.g., capt__n/military rank). The test is timed at 10 minutes.

A sample of 316 undergraduate university students was tested on the Spelling Component Test. Results from this administration were combined with the 386 subjects tested [earlier] to furnish a normative sample of 702 university students (407 females and 295 males).

The normative distribution of scores, for the full sample and separated by gender, is given in Table 3, in terms of cumulative percentages. (See Table 3 on the next page.)

Questions for Exercise 10

Part A: Factual Questions

1. What percentage of the females had scores at and below 27–28?

2. What percentage of the males had scores at and below 27–28?

3. Compare your answers to Questions 1 and 2. Based on these two answers, does it appear that females *or* males performed better on the spelling test? Explain.

---

[1] Source: Coren, S. (1989). The Spelling Component Test: Psychometric evaluation and norms. *Educational and Psychological Measurement, 49*, 961–971. Copyright © 1989 by Educational and Psychological Measurement. Reprinted with permission.

Table 3
Norms for the Spelling Component Test Based on 702 University Undergraduate Students

Raw score	Cumulative Percentage		
	Females (*N* = 407)	Males (*N* = 295)	Total (*N* = 702)
69–70	99.4	99.6	99.5
67–68	98.6	99.6	99.0
65–66	97.1	99.6	98.2
63–64	94.8	97.1	95.9
61–62	92.5	95.5	93.9
59–60	88.0	93.0	90.5
57–58	83.0	87.6	85.2
55–56	76.1	84.7	79.8
53–54	70.9	79.3	74.7
51–52	67.4	76.0	71.4
49–50	63.4	72.3	67.5
47–48	59.0	68.2	63.2
45–46	53.0	61.2	56.7
43–44	45.0	53.3	48.8
41–42	36.9	49.2	42.5
39–40	31.7	43.8	36.8
37–38	25.6	38.2	31.0
35–36	20.5	30.2	25.0
33–34	16.4	24.4	20.4
31–32	11.2	17.8	14.3
29–30	8.1	14.5	11.2
27–28	6.1	11.2	7.9
25–26	4.0	8.7	5.7
23–24	2.0	6.2	3.6
21–22	1.4	4.1	2.5
19–20	0.9	3.7	2.0
17–18	0.3	1.2	1.0
15–16	0.3	0.4	0.3

4. Based on the total sample, what is the percentile rank for a person with a raw score of 34?

5. Based on the norms for males, what is the percentile rank for a male with a raw score of 34?

6. Based on the total sample, a percentile rank of about 85 corresponds to which raw scores?

7. What percentage of the females had scores of 38 or less?

8. What percentage of the males had scores of 38 or less?

9. If the test were being used for college admissions, would a female who had a raw score of 38 be better off if her percentile rank being used for admissions purposes was derived from the female norms *or* the norms for the total sample (both males and females)? Explain.

10. If the test were being used for college admissions, would a male who had a raw score of 38 be better off if his percentile rank being used for admissions purposes was derived from the male norms *or* the norms for the total sample (both males and females)? Explain.

Part B: Questions for Discussion

11. The researcher states that there were 76 words on the test, but the highest score in Table 3 is 70. Speculate on the reason for this apparent discrepancy.

12. Suppose your professor administered the spelling test to you and offered to give you either your raw score only *or* your percentile rank based on your gender only. Which would you choose? Why?

13. The norms for the total sample are based on the responses of more women than men. Is this a problem? Explain.

Exercise 11   Counseling Duration

Mean, Median, Mode, and Cumulative Percentage

Statistical Guide

The mean (M) is the average that is the balance point in a distribution. It is calculated by summing all the scores and dividing by the number of scores. The mean is pulled toward extreme scores in an unbalanced distribution (i.e., a skewed distribution, with extreme scores on one side and without extreme scores on the other side to balance it).

The median (Mdn) is the average that indicates the value below which half of the cases lie. For example, if the median for a group is 10.0, then 50 percent of the cases lie below 10.0. The median is *not* pulled toward extreme scores in a skewed distribution.

The mode is the most frequently occurring score. For instance, if more individuals have a score of 29 than have any other score, then 29 is the mode.

See the previous exercise for the definition of cumulative percentage. A common symbol for cumulative percentage is *cum%*. Because a cumulative percentage is calculated by summing percentages, an alternative symbol is $\Sigma\%$, which is shown in the table in the excerpt. Note that the Greek letter Σ means "sum of" in statistics.

The f in the table in the excerpt means "frequency," which indicates how many had each score.

"Scores" are not always "test scores" in statistics. In the excerpt, the scores are "number of sessions completed." Thus, if a client completes 10 sessions, his or her score is 10. The scores in the table in the excerpt have been "grouped." For instance, "1–3" in the first column in the table represents this group of scores: 1, 2, and 3.

Excerpt from the Research Article[1]

During an academic year, new clients at a university counseling center were recruited to participate in this study. All new clients requesting individual counseling services were eligible to participate. Ninety-four new clients (the majority of new clients at the center) agreed to participate.... The ages of the participants ranged from 18 years to 47 years ($Mdn = 21.00$, $M = 22.4...$).

Table 2 presents a frequency distribution of counseling duration. Participants completed from 1 to 28 sessions ($Mdn = 3.0$, $M = 4.6...$). As evident in the table, most participants completed a relatively small number of sessions.

Table 2
Frequency Distribution of Counseling Duration

No. of sessions completed	f	%	$\Sigma\%$
1–3	54	57.4	57.4
4–6	22	23.4	80.8
7–9	8	8.5	89.3
10–12	4	4.3	93.6
14–17	3	3.2	96.8
18–28	3	3.2	100.0

Note. Mdn = 3, Mode = 1, M = 4.6

---

[1] Source: Hatchett, G. T. (2003). Does psychopathology predict counseling duration? *Psychological Reports*, *93*, 175–185. Copyright © 2003 by Psychological Reports. Reprinted with permission.

Questions for Exercise 11

Part A: Factual Questions

1. What is the median age of the clients?

2. What percentage of clients was under 21 years of age?

3. Are the mean and the median number of sessions completed the same? Explain.

4. The footnote to the table states: "Mode = 1." What does this mean?

5. How many clients completed 7–9 sessions?

6. What percentage of the clients completed 7–9 sessions?

7. What is the cumulative percentage for 7–9 sessions?

8. What percentage completed between 1 and 9 sessions?

9. Which group of scores has the highest percentage of clients?

10. Is the following statement true *or* false?
"57.4% of the clients completed more than 1 to 3 sessions."

11. Is the following statement true *or* false?

    "100% of the clients completed between 18 and 28 sessions."

12. Is the following statement true *or* false?

    "80.8% of the clients completed six or fewer sessions."

Part B: Questions for Discussion

13. The researcher states that "most participants completed a relatively small number of sessions." Do the statistics in the table in the excerpt support this statement? Explain.

14. Consider the frequencies (f) in the table. In your opinion, is the distribution clearly skewed? Explain.

15. The researcher chose to group the scores in the first column (i.e., 1–3, 4–6, and so on). An alternative would be to list all the scores individually in the first column (i.e., 1, 2, 3, 4, 5, and so on) without grouping. If you had prepared the table, would you have grouped the scores? Why? Why not?

Exercise 12   Injection Drug Users and HIV
Median and Interquartile Range: I

Statistical Guide

To review the median, see the statistical guide for Exercise 11.

The interquartile range indicates the scores obtained by the middle 50 percent of the participants. Put another way, if all the scores are put in order from low to high and the bottom 25 percent and the top 25 percent are temporarily ignored, the range of the remaining scores is the interquartile range. This statistic is a measure of *variability* (also known as *spread* or *dispersion*) that is usually reported in conjunction with the median.

Excerpt from the Research Article[1]

This analysis was conducted as part of the World Health Organization (WHO) Multi-Centre Study of AIDS and Injecting Drug Use. Persons who had injected illicit drugs within the previous 2 months were recruited from drug abuse treatment programs and nontreatment settings (in most cities, through outreach and chain-referral sampling). It is estimated that at least 95% of the subjects who were asked to participate agreed to do so.

The questionnaire focused on drug use histories and on injection and sexual risk behavior in the 6 months prior to the interview.... After the interview, either a blood or saliva specimen was obtained for HIV testing.

A specific series of questions was used to ascertain subjects' deliberate behavioral changes in response to concerns about AIDS. Subjects were asked, "Since you first heard about AIDS, have you done anything to avoid getting AIDS?" Those who responded "yes," that they had changed their behavior, were then asked, "What have you done?"

In each of the four cities [in Table 1], changes in drug injection behavior were reported more often than changes in sexual behavior. The most commonly reported risk reduction was the "stopped/reduced sharing" of injection equipment. The most commonly reported sexual risk reductions were an increased use of condoms, greater selectivity in choosing sexual partners, and a reduced number of sexual partners.

Table 1
Demographic Characteristics, Reported AIDS Risk Reduction, and HIV Seroprevalence Among Injection Drug Users by City

City	Median Age (Interquartile Range)	Male %	Median Education (Interquartile Range)	Median Years Injecting (Interquartile Range)	Reported Risk Reduction %	HIV Positive %
Bangkok (n = 590)	30 (25–33)	95	7 (4–10)	8 (3.5–13)	92	34
Glasgow (n = 452)	23 (21–26)	70	11 (10–11)	6 (4–8)	83	2
New York (n = 829)	37 (31–41)	76	11 (10–12)	19 (10–24)	79	48
Rio de Janeiro (n = 128)	30 (25–33)	83	12 (9–14.5)	10 (4.5–14)	58	35

[1] Source: Des Jarlais, D. C., Friedmann, P., Hagan, H., & Friedman, S. R. (1996). The protective effect of AIDS-related behavioral change among injection drug users: A cross-national study. *American Journal of Public Health, 86,* 1780–1785. Copyright © by the American Public Health Association. Reprinted with permission.

Questions for Exercise 12

Part A: Factual Questions

1. On the average, the participants in which city were oldest? Explain.

2. In Bangkok, what percentage of the participants had less than 7 years of education?

3. In New York, what percentage of the participants had more than 11 years of education?

4. On the average, the participants in which city had the fewest years of injecting?

5. The participants in which city had the greatest variability in their ages? Explain.

6. The participants in which city had the greatest dispersion in their number of years of education?

7. In New York, what percentage of the participants had been injecting for 10 to 24 years?

8. In New York, what percentage of the participants had been injecting for less than 10 years?

9. In New York, *how many* of the 829 participants had been injecting for more than 24 years?

10. In Rio de Janeiro, what percentage of the participants had been injecting from 4.5 to 14 years?

11. In Rio de Janeiro, *how many* of the 128 participants had been injecting for more than 14 years?

12. The participants in which city had the least variability in the number of years of injecting?

Part B: Questions for Discussion

13. Many textbook authors suggest that the interquartile range be reported as a single value obtained by subtracting the two values shown in the excerpt. For example, in the excerpt, the interquartile range is shown as "25–33" for the median age of Bangkok's participants. Using the textbook authors' suggestion, it would be reported as "8" (i.e., 33 – 25 = 8). Which method of reporting do you prefer? Why?

14. The median age of the participants in New York is substantially higher than in the other cities. Could this help explain some of the differences in median years of injecting across cities? Explain.

15. The city with the lowest percentage of HIV+ participants had the lowest median age. Does this make sense? Explain.

16. When considering data on HIV risk reduction behavior, would you be interested in an analysis that considers men and women separately? Explain.

17. Speculate on what the authors mean by "chain-referral sampling."

Exercise 13 Adolescent Physical Abuse and Suicide

Median and Interquartile Range: II

Statistical Guide

To review the median and interquartile range, see the statistical guides for Exercises 11 and 12.

To obtain the interquartile range, you must identify the 25th percentile (the score below which 25% of the participants scored) and the 75th percentile (the score below which 75% of the participants scored).

Note that in this excerpt the authors refer to *significant differences*. You will be learning about this topic in detail later in this book. At this point, *significant differences* may be thought of as *reliable differences*. Usually, significant differences are large enough to be of interest in the interpretation of results.

Excerpt from the Research Article[1]

The sample, representing a white, middle-class, suburban population, consisted of 99 physically abused adolescents from Nassau and Suffolk Counties…. [Adolescents who had suffered intrafamilial *sexual* abuse were not included in the sample of 99 abused adolescents.]

In the abuse sample, biological fathers were most frequently indicated as the perpetrators of adolescent abuse (73% of the cases). Mothers were indicated as perpetrators in 25% of the cases. Stepfathers were indicated as the perpetrators in 10% of the cases. In 10 families, more than one perpetrator was indicated.

For this study, a suicide attempt was defined as any intentional, self-inflicted injury accompanied by a statement of suicidal intent, or classic severe suicidal injuries such as a large ingestion of toxic substances (e.g., 20 pills or more at one time), self-inflicted deep wounds to wrist or throat, unsuccessful hanging, or gunshot wounds to the head or abdomen.

[The Family Adaptability and Cohesion Scale] is a 20-item, paper-and-pencil self-report measure…. [For this scale,] cohesion is defined as "the emotional bonding that family members have toward each other"…and adaptability is defined as "the ability of a marital or family system to change its power structure, role relationships, and relationship rules in response to situational and developmental stress." [Higher scores indicate more cohesion and more adaptability.]

[Academic performance was measured with the Youth Self-Report. In the national norm group, the mean score for academic performance was 50.]

Table 1 presents comparative data on indicators of adolescent vulnerability leading to mental illness and suicidal behavior. Abused attempters were not significantly different from abused nonattempters in peer social support: No significant differences were found in either the number of close friends they cited or reported they enjoyed being with. However, they reported inadequacies in family support. Abused attempters perceived their mothers as being less caring (median = 16.5) than did abused nonattempters (median = 29)…and they perceived their families to be less cohesive (median = 20.5) than did abused nonattempters (median = 24).

---

[1] Source: Kaplan, S. J., Pelcovitz, D., Salzinger, S., Mandel, F., & Weiner, M. (1997). Adolescent physical abuse and suicide attempts. *Journal of the American Academy of Child and Adolescent Psychiatry, 36,* 799–808. Copyright © 1997 by Williams & Wilkins. Reprinted with permission.

Table 1
Indices of Vulnerability in Abused Attempters and Abused Nonattempters

	Attempters		Nonattempters	
	Median	IQR	Median	IQR
Peers				
No. of close friends	3	0–4	4	1–8
No. of peers enjoy	2.5	0–3.5	4	1–7
Family				
Perception of mother's caring	16.5	13.0–27.5	29	20–32
Perception of father's caring	14.5	6.5–21.5	19.5	14–26
Family cohesion	20.5	17.5–26	24	23–25
Family adaptability	24	19.0–25.5	22	10–26
Academic performance				
YSR score	35	30–47	42	35–51

Note. IQR = interquartile range (25th to 75th percentile); YSR = Youth Self-Report

Questions for Exercise 13

Part A: Factual Questions

1. On the average, which group reported having more close friends?

2. On the average, which group reported having lower academic performance?

3. What percentage of the nonattempters reported having between 1 and 8 close friends?

4. What percentage of the nonattempters reported having more than 8 close friends?

5. What percentage of the attempters reported having more than 4 close friends?

6. What is the 75th percentile for "No. of close friends" for nonattempters?

7. What is the 25th percentile for "No. of close friends" for nonattempters?

8. Which group was more variable in the "No. of close friends"? Explain.

9. Which group was less variable in "Family cohesion"? Explain.

10. Did any of the middle 50% of attempters have a "YSR score" as high as the national mean of 50?

11. What is the average difference between the two groups in "Family cohesion" scores?

12. What is the median difference between the two groups in "Perception of mother's caring"?

Part B: Questions for Discussion

13. Speculate on why adolescents who had been sexually abused were not included in the study.

14. If you have a statistics textbook, examine the definition of the interquartile range. Are the inter-quartile ranges in this excerpt reported as suggested in your textbook? (Hint: For each variable in the excerpt, the IQR is reported as two score values.) Explain.

15. The authors chose to report the median and interquartile range instead of the mean and standard deviation. If you have a statistics textbook, examine it to determine under what circumstances this is recommended. Write your findings here.

Exercise 14   Mental Health Contact Hours

Mean, Median, and Histogram

Statistical Guide

See the statistical guide for Exercise 7 to review the purpose of a histogram. See the statistical guide for Exercise 11 to review the meaning of the mean and median and their relationship to skewed distributions. The mean and median are both "measures of central tendency." Measures of central tendency are also called "averages."

Small numbers of scores that are far from the bulk of the scores are called "outliers."

A distribution with extreme scores to the right (but not the left) is said to have a positive skew, while one with extreme scores to the left is said to have a negative skew.

Excerpt from the Research Article[1]

This study surveyed a sample of...mental health professionals employed by two community mental health agencies in rural northern and central Michigan.... The survey sample included social workers (65.8%), psychologists (11%), counselors (8.2%), and other professionals (4%).

Figure 1 demonstrates that community mental health professionals reported 0 to 16 hr/week of family contact time. The mean of reported family contact hours per week was 3.5; the mean was 3.02 with two large outliers omitted. Given the large positive skew of the distribution..., a useful measure of central tendency is the median of 2 hr/week of reported family contact time. The average number of hours per week of family contact time for professionals who served children was 7.39; the average number of hours per week of family contact time for professionals who served adults was 2.58.

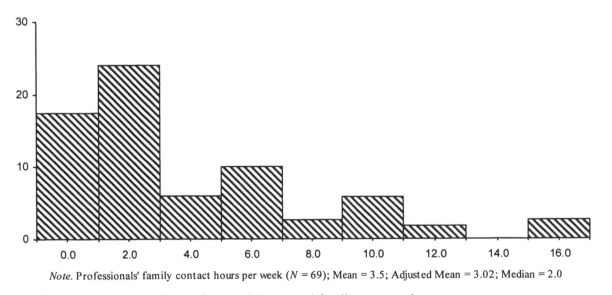

Note. Professionals' family contact hours per week (N = 69); Mean = 3.5; Adjusted Mean = 3.02; Median = 2.0

Figure 1. Mental health professionals' reported family contact time.

---

[1] Source: Riebschleger, J. (2005). Mental health professionals' contact with family members of people with psychiatric disabilities. *Families in Society: The Journal of Contemporary Social Services, 86*, 9–16. Copyright © 2005 by the Alliance for Children and Families. Reprinted with permission.

Questions for Exercise 14

Part A: Factual Questions

1. What is the sample size?

2. In the histogram, are the outliers "far to the left" *or* "far to the right"?

3. By how many points do the mean of 3.5 and the median differ?

4. How have the outliers influenced the mean?

5. What percentage of participants reported less than 2.0 contact hours? Explain the basis for your answer.

6. Is the distribution in the histogram skewed? Explain.

Part B: Questions for Discussion

7. Do you think that the mean of 3.5 or the median of 2.0 is better for describing the average of the distribution in the histogram? Explain.

8. What kind of information does the "adjusted mean" provide that the mean of 3.5 does not provide?

9. In the last sentence, the researcher reports two averages (7.39 and 2.58). Which average do you think was reported: the "mean" *or* the "median"?

10. The sample included various subgroups of mental health professionals (e.g., social workers and psychologists). In your opinion, would it have been more informative to provide separate histograms for each type of professional?

Exercise 15   Cancer Risk-Reduction Behaviors

Mean and Range

Statistical Guide

See the statistical guide for Exercise 11 to review the definition of the mean.

The range is the difference between the highest score and the lowest score in a set of scores. (Some statisticians add "1" to the difference.) Sometimes researchers merely report the highest and lowest values (without subtracting) and refer to the two values as the range. The range is an indicator of the variation in a set of scores. *Variation* is sometimes referred to as *dispersion* or *spread*.

Background Notes

The researchers who reported the information below were studying the physical activity behaviors of women who had survived breast cancer. The women in the study self-reported their levels of physical activity (i.e., their activities were *not* observed by the researchers).

Excerpt from the Research Article[1]

Although more time was reported for light physical activities, most were fairly physically active with the exception of engaging in activities that were rated as being hard or very hard (see the table).

Table 1
Physical Activity (Mean Hours/Day Averaged over 7 Days)

Activity Level	M	Range
Sleep	7.35	5.5–8.8
Light physical activity	8.71	3.0–16.0
Moderate physical activity	3.36	.71–8.3
Hard physical activity	.78	0–4.1
Very hard physical activity	.14	0–1.05

Questions for Exercise 15

Part A: Factual Questions

1. On the average, how many hours per day did the women sleep?

---

[1] Source: Lindsey, A. M., Waltman, N., Gross, G., Ott, C. D., & Twiss, J. (2004). Cancer risk-reduction behaviors of breast cancer survivors. *Western Journal of Nursing Research*, *26*, 872–890. Copyright © 2004 by Sage Publications. Reprinted with permission.

2. On the average, how many hours a day did the women engage in "Light physical activity"?

3. On the average, which type of physical activity was engaged in for the fewest number of hours?

4. Did the women average more than an hour a day of "Hard physical activity"?

5. Did the women average more than an hour a day of "Moderate physical activity"?

6. What is the smallest number of hours of sleep reported?

7. Did some of the women report engaging in no "Hard physical activity"? Explain.

8. Did any of the women report engaging in more than an hour of "Hard physical activity"? Explain.

9. Is there more variation in "Hard physical activity" *or* in "Very hard physical activity"? Explain.

Part B: Questions for Discussion

10. In your opinion, are there advantages and disadvantages to using self-reports for gathering data on physical activities instead of directly observing the participants' activities? Explain.

11. The women were asked about their activities over a seven-day period. In your opinion, is this a long enough period of time? Explain.

Exercise 16   Self-Reported Height and Weight

Mean, Standard Deviation, and 68% Rule

Statistical Guide

To review the mean, see the statistical guide for Exercise 11.

The standard deviation is a yardstick for measuring variability (i.e., differences among participants, subjects, respondents, or cases). Synonyms for *variability* are *spread* and *dispersion*. The larger the value of the standard deviation, the greater the variability.

In a normal distribution (i.e., a type of symmetrical, bell-shaped distribution), about 34% of the cases lie one standard deviation unit on either side of the mean. For example, if the mean equals 50.00 for a normal distribution and one standard deviation unit equals 10.00, then 68% of the cases lie within (i.e., plus and minus) 10 points of the mean (i.e., 68% lies between 40.00 and 60.00).

Excerpt from the Research Article[1]

Accuracy in height and weight characteristics allows accuracy in calculating placement in health categories. Typically, questionnaires on health-risk appraisal and insurance applications require participants to include their [own estimates]....

A convenience sample of 62 ($n = 30$ men, $n = 32$ women) Euro-American college students with a mean age of 19.9 years ($SD = 2.9$) volunteered for the study.

Subjects were asked to volunteer for a simple assessment of fitness behavior via questionnaire, which included items of height and weight, but were not told prior to completing the survey that height and weight would be measured [using a scale]. Heights and weights were measured to the nearest 0.125 in. (0.0032 m) and 0.25 lb. (0.113 kg) and were converted to meters and kilograms, respectively.

Table 1

Comparison of Self-Reported and Measured Height and Weight for College Men
(n = 30) and Women (n = 32)

Condition		M	SD
Men	Self-reported height, m	1.79	0.07
	Measured height, m	1.78	0.06
Women	Self-reported height, m	1.62	0.07
	Measured height, m	1.62	0.07
Men	Self-reported weight, kg	79.70	13.39
	Measured weight, kg	79.20	14.44
Women	Self-reported weight, kg	61.20	9.06
	Measured weight, kg	63.10	10.02

These data agree with the majority of previous findings in that both men and women exhibit inaccuracies in self-reporting physical characteristics. In contrast, however, the majority of previous studies showed that both men and women tended to underreport weight and overreport height.

---

[1] Source: Jacobson, B. H., & DeBock, D. H. (2001). Comparison of body mass index by self-reported versus measured height and weight. *Perceptual and Motor Skills, 92,* 128–132. Copyright © 2001 by Perceptual and Motor Skills. Reprinted with permission.

Questions for Exercise 16

Part A: Factual Questions

1. What was the average age of the students?

2. Assuming that the distribution of age is normal, what percentage of students was between 17.0 and 22.8 years?

3. On the average, was the "Self-reported weight" for men higher *or* lower than their measured weight?

4. For weight, did men *or* women have a larger average difference between "Self-reported weight" and "Measured weight"?

5. Did men *or* women have greater variability in their "Self-reported weight"?

6. For men, was there greater dispersion for "Self-reported weight" *or* for "Measured weight"?

7. Assuming that the distribution of "Self-reported height" for men is normal, the middle 68% of the men had scores between what two values?

8. Assuming that the distribution of "Self-reported weight" for women is normal, what percentage of the women reported weights between 61.20 and 70.26 kg?

9. Assuming that the distribution of "Self-reported weight" for women is normal, what percentage of the women reported weights between 52.14 and 70.26 kg?

10. Assuming that the distribution of "Self-reported height" for women is normal, what percentage reported heights between 1.55 and 1.62 m?

11. Assuming that the distribution of "Measured weight" for women is normal, the middle 68% of the women had scores between what two values?

Part B: Questions for Discussion

12. Before reading the results in the excerpt, would you have predicted that self-reports and measured values of height and weight would differ? Explain.

13. Two methods (self-report and a scale) were used to measure weight. In your opinion, is one method inherently better than the other? Explain.

14. The researchers note a difference in the pattern of results in this study and the pattern in the majority of other studies on this topic. Before reaching a conclusion on this topic, how interested would you be in examining the other studies? Explain.

Exercise 17   College Students' Procrastination

Mean, Standard Deviation, and Approximate 95% and 99.7% Rules

Statistical Guide

To review the mean, see the statistical guide for Exercise 11. To review the standard deviation, see the statistical guide for Exercise 16.

If you go out 2 standard deviation units on both sides of the mean, you capture approximately the middle 95% of the cases in a normal distribution. (The precise rule for capturing 95% of the cases is given in the next exercise.) If you go out 3 standard deviations on both sides on the mean, you capture 99.7% of the cases.

Excerpt from the Research Article[1]

The Procrastination Log [PL]…was administered both at intake [pretest to a one-hour individual counseling session on procrastination] and on outtake [posttest]. The PL is the most widely used instrument for assessing difficulties with procrastination…. It is a 9-item self-report questionnaire that measures procrastination-related behavior during the past week. The instrument lists nine common behaviors associated with procrastination (e.g., "I went out when I should have been studying") and asks participants to rate each item on a 7-point Likert-type scale ranging from 1 (*true*) to 7 (*false*). [Higher scores indicate a higher degree of procrastination.]

After participants agreed to be involved in the study, they were randomly assigned to one of three experimental groups…. [In the "same-attribution" group, the counselor agreed with the participants' attributions for their procrastination behavior such as bad luck, fate, family of origin, and biology. In the "no-attribution group," the counselor said that no attributions were necessary to find a solution to the problem. In the "different-attribution group," the counselor attributed the cause of procrastination to a cause other than the one the participant attributed it to.]

The major finding of the current study was that, contrary to prediction, [the group given the intervention that offered no causal explanation outperformed the other two groups].

Table 1
*Group Means and Standard Deviations [of Procrastination Log (PL) scores]**

Group	Intake		Outtake	
	M	*SD*	*M*	*SD*
Same-attribution group (*n* = 27)	43.5	8.6	37.4	9.1
No-attribution group (*n* = 28)	45.7	5.9	33.4	10.8
Different-attribution group (*n* = 27)	41.9	10.7	36.8	9.2

*Higher scores indicate greater self-reported procrastination.

---

[1] Source: Cook, P. F. (2000). Effects of counselors' etiology attributions on college students' procrastination. *Journal of Counseling Psychology, 47,* 352–361. Copyright © 2000 by the American Psychological Association. Reprinted with permission.

Questions for Exercise 17

Part A: Factual Questions

1. On the average, which group had higher scores on "Intake"?

2. At "Intake," which group had the greatest variability in their scores?

3. At "Intake," which group had the least variability in their scores?

4. On the average, which group showed the greatest improvement from "Intake" to "Outtake"?

5. Assuming that the distribution of PL scores for the "No-attribution group" at "Intake" is normal, between what two values did approximately the middle 95% of the participants lie?

6. Does the mean "Intake" score for the "Same-attribution group" fall within the range of the two scores that you gave as your answer to Question 5?

7. Assuming that the distribution of PL scores for the "No-attribution group" at "Outtake" is normal, between what two values did approximately the middle 95% of the participants lie?

8. Assuming that the distribution of scores for the "No-attribution group" at "Outtake" is normal, between what two values did the middle 99.7% of the participants lie?

9. For the "Different-attribution group" at "Outtake," what percentage of the students had scores between 9.2 and 64.4?

Part B: Questions for Discussion

10. If your work is correct, the interval you calculated for Question 8 should be larger than the interval you calculated for Question 7. Does this make sense? Explain.

11. If you are a procrastinator, do you think that a one-hour counseling session would be of help to you? Explain.

12. Some participants might report what they think the experimenters expect them to report. For example, after treatment for phobia of snakes, participants might report less phobia after treatment only because they believe that the experimenter would like to have that outcome. Do you think that this type of problem might be present in this particular study? Explain.

13. Is it important to know that the PL is the "most widely used instrument for assessing difficulties with procrastination"? Explain.

Exercise 18   Competitiveness and Culture
Mean, Standard Deviation, and Precise 95% and 99% Rules

Statistical Guide

To review the mean, see the statistical guide for Exercise 11. To review the standard deviation, see the statistical guide for Exercise 16. Note that a small standard deviation indicates that a group is *homogeneous*, while a large standard deviation indicates that a group is *heterogeneous*.

If you go out 1.96 standard deviation units on both sides of the mean in a normal distribution, you capture 95% of the cases. (In the previous exercise, the approximate 95% rule was given.)

If you go out 2.58 standard deviation units on both sides of the mean in a normal distribution, you capture 99% of the cases.

Excerpt from the Research Article[1]

A total of 454 undergraduates (61 Chinese, 232 Japanese, and 161 American), [attending universities in their respective countries] participated.

All participants completed the revised Competitiveness Index.... The index uses a 5-point...response format anchored by 1: Strongly Disagree and 5: Strongly Agree. Examples of scale items include "I enjoy competing against an opponent," and "I often remain quiet rather than risk hurting another person."

Table 1
Means and Standard Deviations for Age and Competitiveness Scores

Measure	China		Japan		United States		Total	
	M	SD	M	SD	M	SD	M	SD
Age, yr.								
Women	21.2	1.8	20.6	0.1	19.6	1.6	20.3	1.5
Men	20.8	0.8	20.1	1.0	20.6	1.6	20.4	1.2
Total	21.0	1.4	20.4	1.0	20.0	1.6		
Enjoyment of competition								
Women	29.3	7.1	27.6	6.2	31.2	9.4	29.4	8.0
Men	30.8	8.1	30.1	6.2	36.6	6.4	32.1	7.1
Total	30.1	7.6	29.0	6.3	33.4	8.7		
Contentiousness								
Women	14.4	4.4	14.8	3.0	14.7	4.6	14.7	4.0
Men	15.6	4.1	14.5	3.1	15.9	4.4	15.1	3.7
Total	15.0	4.2	14.6	3.0	15.2	4.6		

[1] Source: Houston, J. M., Harris, P. B., Moore, R., Brummett, R., & Kametani, H. (2005). Competitiveness among Japanese, Chinese, and American undergraduate students. *Psychological Reports*, *97*, 205–212. Copyright © 2005 by Psychological Reports. Reprinted with permission.

Questions for Exercise 18

Part A: Factual Questions

1. The table contains means and standard deviations. Which one of these statistics indicates the amount of variability within each national-origin group?

   A. Mean   B. Standard Deviation

2. Examine the statistics for "Enjoyment of competition" for men. Which national-origin group has the most variability in its scores? Explain the basis for your answer.

3. Examine the statistics for "Enjoyment of competition" for men. Which national-origin group has the highest mean score? Explain the basis for your answer.

4. The mean age for the total Chinese sample is 21.0. Assuming that the age distribution is normal, the middle 95% of the cases lies between what two ages? (Use the multiplier given in the statistical guide for this exercise. Round your answer to one decimal place.)

5. The mean age for the total Japan sample is 20.4. Assuming that the age distribution is normal, the middle 95% of the cases lies between what two ages? (Round your answer to one decimal place.)

6. The mean age for men in the China sample is 20.8. Assuming that the distribution of these scores is normal, the middle 99% of the cases lies between what two ages? (Round your answer to one decimal place.)

7. The mean score for women on "Contentiousness" for the Japan sample is 14.8. Assuming that the distribution of these scores is normal, the middle 99% of the cases lies between what two scores? (Round your answer to one decimal place.)

8. The mean score on "Contentiousness" for all women is 14.7. Assuming that the distribution of these scores is normal, what percentage of the cases have scores between 6.9 and 22.5?

9. Overall, which national-origin group is most homogeneous in its level of "Contentiousness"? Explain your answer.

10. The women in which sample are the most heterogeneous in their level of "Enjoyment of competition"? Explain.

    A. The China sample
    B. The Japan sample
    C. The United States sample

Part B: Questions for Discussion

11. Consider Questions 2 and 3. If your answers are correct, one national origin group has a higher standard deviation while a different group has a higher mean. Does this surprise you? Explain.

12. The authors of the excerpt did not state whether the distributions of scores were normally distributed. (This is true of most research writers in the social and behavioral sciences; it is traditional *not* to address normality in their research reports.) Does this pose a problem for consumers of research? Explain.

Exercise 19   Problems of Students Absent from School

T Score: I

Statistical Guide

T scores have a mean of 50.00 and a standard deviation of 10.00 for the norm group on which a new test is standardized. Test makers prepare norms tables that allow us to convert a person's raw score (points earned) to the *T* score equivalents that would have been obtained if that person had been in the norm group. Likewise, we can compare the mean and standard deviation of another group to the mean of 50.00 and standard deviation of 10.00 for the norm group.

Since there are about 3 standard deviation units on both sides of the mean in a normal distribution, in practice, *T* scores can range from 20.00 to 80.00 (i.e., 3 times the standard deviation of 10.00 ± the mean of 50.00).

Note that the mean of 50.00 and the standard deviation of 10.00 are true of the *norm group* but not necessarily true of a subsequent group that is studied. Hence, if a study group has a mean of 55.00, the reader will immediately know that their mean is higher than the norm group's mean. Also, for instance, if the study group's standard deviation is 9.00, the reader will immediately know that their standard deviation is lower than the norm group's standard deviation.

Excerpt from the Research Article[1]

Subjects consisted of 44 adolescents (17 males and 27 females) 12 to 18 years of age [who had a] minimum of 20% absences from school in the 4 weeks prior to evaluation for the study. [On average, they missed 72% of full or partial school days.] Subjects were recruited through biannual mailings sent to middle, junior high, and high schools in the seven-county metropolitan area surrounding Minneapolis and St. Paul. Referrals were made by school personnel, physicians, mental health workers, and family members.

Child Behavior Checklist. The CBCL is a report measure that the parent completes about the child…. There are eight scales of the CBCL (Withdrawn, Somatic Complaints [i.e., medical complaints about the body], Anxious/Depressed, Social Problems, Thought Problems, Attention Problems, Delinquent Behavior, and Aggressive Behavior). *T* scores of 70 (98th percentile) or greater are considered clinically significant.

In reporting their adolescents' symptoms on the CBCL, mothers endorsed the Somatic Complaints scale as having the highest mean ($T = 72.5 \pm 11.4$) (Table 1). The next highest group mean scores were on the Anxious/Depressed scale ($T = 70.4 \pm 10.7$) and the Withdrawn scale ($T = 69.8 \pm 10.6$).

---

[1] Source: Bernstein, G. A., Massie, E. D., Thuras, P. D., Perwien, A. R., Borchardt, C. M., & Crosby, R. D. (1997). Somatic symptoms in anxious-depressed school refusers. *Journal of the American Academy of Child and Adolescent Psychiatry*, *36*, 661–668. Copyright © 1997 by Williams & Wilkins. Reprinted with permission.

Table 1
CBCL Scores Reported by Mothers

| | *T* scores | |
Scales	Mean	*SD*
Withdrawn	69.8	10.6
Somatic Complaints	72.5	11.4
Anxious/Depressed	70.4	10.7
Social Problems	62.6	11.8
Thought Problems	60.0	8.7
Attention Problems	64.1	7.9
Delinquent Behavior	63.1	7.3
Aggressive Behavior	61.0	9.2

Questions for Exercise 19

Part A: Factual Questions

1. On which scale did the adolescents in this study have the lowest average score?

2. On which scale did the adolescents in this study have the most variability in their scores?

3. Suppose you were able to examine the scores of the individuals in this study. On which scale would you expect to find the largest differences among the scores of the adolescents? Explain.

4. Is the mean score for the adolescents in this study on the "Anxious/Depressed" scale above *or* below the mean for the norm group? Describe the basis for your answer.

5. On how many of the scales is the mean for the adolescents in this study above the mean for the norm group?

6. On which scales is the mean score for adolescents in this study in the "clinically significant" area? (See the excerpt for the definition of "clinically significant.")

7. Is it likely that some of the individual adolescents in this study had "clinically significant" scores on the "Withdrawn" scale? Explain.

8. Is it likely that some of the individual adolescents in this study had scores lower than 70 on the "Somatic Complaints" scale? Explain.

9. Assuming that the distribution of scores on the "Delinquent Behavior" scale for the adolescents in this study is normal, the middle 68% had scores between what two values?

10. Assuming that the distribution of scores on the "Delinquent Behavior" score *for the adolescents in the norm group* is normal, the middle 68% had scores between what two values?

Part B: Questions for Discussion

11. Compare your answers to Questions 9 and 10. Based on the performance of the middle 68% on the "Delinquent Behavior" scale, would you be willing to say that the adolescents in this study are clearly higher than those in the norm group? Explain.

12. In your opinion, would it be a good idea to arrange the scales in Table 1 alphabetically? Explain.

13. The authors discuss only some of the values from Table 1 in their discussion of the table. In your opinion, is this appropriate, or should they have discussed each of the values?

14. Many researchers report the means and standard deviations of raw scores (i.e., points earned) rather than derived scores such as *T* scores. Which is more helpful to you when interpreting the statistics? Explain.

Exercise 20 Effects of Exercise on Mood

T Score: II

Statistical Guide

To review *T* scores, see the statistical guide for Exercise 19.

The *T* score norms for the scale used in this exercise were derived from the performance of 3,361 participants from age 12 to 39 years. The raw scores of this norm group were converted into *T* scores and placed in a norms table. The raw scores of participants in this study were converted to *T* scores using the norms table. Then, the mean *T* scores and standard deviations for the entire group were calculated for analysis (see Table 1 in the excerpt).

Excerpt from the Research Article[1]

The purpose of this study was to investigate mood changes following participation in the same exercise session performed twice with one week apart…. The exercise session took place at the same time of day on the same day each week. The session was a resistance-training session.

Mood was assessed using the 24-item Brunel University Mood Scale (BRUMS)…. The measure assesses Anger, Confusion, Depression, Fatigue, Tension, and Vigor. …scores on the BRUMS [were] transformed into standard *T*-score format ($M = 50.00$, $SD = 10.00$) [for the norm group].

Table 1
Comparison of Profile of Mood T Scores Before and After Exercise over Two Sessions

Mood	Pre-exercise 1		Post-exercise 1		Pre-exercise 2		Post-exercise 2	
	M	*SD*	*M*	*SD*	*M*	*SD*	*M*	*SD*
Anger	45.22	3.86	45.34	3.41	46.09	4.82	45.34	3.41
Confusion	43.04	2.29	42.41	3.83	42.55	2.21	42.49	3.84
Depression	45.04	3.99	43.41	0.31	45.03	3.61	43.72	0.77
Fatigue	41.75	4.14	43.77	3.02	43.66	4.36	45.26	6.24
Tension	43.17	4.22	42.43	2.18	44.19	4.95	42.43	2.18
Vigor	51.70	7.55	52.02	7.57	49.50	9.41	49.85	11.98

Questions for Exercise 20

Part A: Factual Questions

1. Do any of the means for the group in this study exceed the norm group mean? If yes, which one or ones?

---

[1] Source: Lane, A. M., Crone-Grant, D., & Lane, H. (2002). Mood changes following exercise. *Perceptual and Motor Skills*, *94*, 732–734. Copyright © 2002 by Perceptual and Motor Skills. Reprinted with permission.

2. On Post-exercise 2, the mean for which variable comes closest to the norm group mean?

3. What is the difference between the Pre-exercise 1 mean for "Fatigue" and the Post-exercise 1 mean for "Fatigue"?

4. For which "mood" was the difference between the Pre-exercise 1 and Post-exercise 1 means the smallest? (That is, for which variable was there the smallest mean difference?)

5. Is it likely that any of the participants had scores about the norm group mean of 50.00 for "Vigor" on Pre-exercise 2? Explain.

6. Are any of the standard deviations larger than the standard deviation in the norm group? If yes, which one or ones?

7. Which one of the standard deviations in Table 1 is most different from the standard deviation of the norm group?

8. Assume that the distribution of scores on "Vigor" for Pre-exercise 1 is normal. What percentage of the participants in this study had scores between 44.15 and 59.25?

Part B: Questions for Discussion

9. Overall, would you say that the participants in this study were higher *or* lower on average than the norm group for the BRUMS? Explain.

10. The researchers state that "The session was a resistance-training session." Would you like to know more about this exercise session? Explain.

11. If you had planned this study, would you have predicted (i.e., hypothesized) that the mean *T* score for "Depression" would go down from pre-exercise to post-exercise? Explain.

Exercise 21 Exercise and Depression

Effect Size (*d*): I

Statistical Guide

The change from pretest to posttest can be obtained by subtracting the posttest mean from the pretest mean. Unfortunately, this difference is influenced by the scale used to measure the variable of interest. For instance, if one researcher uses a 10-point attitude scale, the largest possible difference is 10 points. In contrast, if another researcher measures the same attitude using a 100-point scale, the largest possible difference is 100 points. Thus, the results of the two studies are not directly comparable.

To standardize differences of the type being considered, researchers sometimes express the difference with a measure of effect size (*d*). While there are variations, the basic formula calls for the difference between the two means to be divided by the standard deviation of the pretest scores. The result is *d*, which indicates the number of standard deviation units by which the pretest mean differs from the posttest mean. Because standard deviation units usually vary from only –3.00 to +3.00, the result will usually be between these two values, regardless of the number of points on the scale that a researcher uses. Here are two examples:

Example 1: Using a 10-point scale, a researcher obtains a pretest mean of 5 and a posttest mean of 7, for a difference of 2 points. The standard deviation of the pretest scores is 3. Dividing 2 by 3 yields 0.67, which is the value of *d*. This indicates that the posttest score exceeds the pretest score by a little more than six-tenths of a standard deviation.

Example 2: Using a 100-point scale, a researcher obtains a pretest mean of 30 and a posttest mean of 36, for a difference of 6 points. The standard deviation of the pretest scores is 10. Dividing 6 by 10 yields 0.60, which is the value of *d*. This indicates that the posttest score exceeds the pretest score by six-tenths of a standard deviation.

The two examples indicate that the results of the two studies are similar, even though scales with very different numbers of points were used.

While there is some controversy on attaching labels to effect sizes, it is common to interpret an effect size (*d*) of 0.5 standard deviation units or greater as being "large," effect sizes of 0.3 to 0.5 as being "moderate," effect sizes of 0.1 to 0.3 as being "small," and effect sizes of less than 0.1 as "trivial."

Note that if *d* equals zero, there is no effect. A *positive* value of *d* indicates that the average posttest score is *higher* than the average pretest score. In contrast, a *negative* value of *d* indicates that the average posttest score is *lower* than the average pretest score. The further the value of *d* is from zero (either in the positive or negative direction), the stronger the effect. The strength of the effect is not affected by whether it is positive or negative. In other words, an effect size of –0.5 or more in the negative direction is also a "large" effect.

Background Notes

A researcher conducted two experiments on the effects of exercise and depression. The participants in the first study were adults who were above average in depression. The participants in the second study were 9- to 12-year-old students enrolled in an after-school exercise program.

Excerpts from the Research Articles[1]

Study 1:

 Participants were recruited from a large corporation.... Those desiring to begin an exercise program were designated exercise participants [the treatment group], and those not desiring to begin exercise at the present time were designated control participants. ...the exercise group consisted of 26 participants and the control group of 24.

 Exercise participants were given a 10-week cardiovascular exercise program consisting of three 20- to 30-minute sessions per week.

 The Profile of Mood States–Short Form Depression Scale requires users to respond to five one-word items (sad, gloomy, lonely, unworthy, discouraged) on a 5-point scale anchored by 0 = Not at All and 4 = Extremely, to indicate "how you have been feeling during the past week including today."

Table 1
Profile of Mood States–Short Form Depression Scale: Mean Scores at 1 and 10 Weeks

Group	*n*	Week 1		Week 10		*d*
		M	*SD*	*M*	*SD*	
Control	24	10.9	3.8	11.1	5.5	.05
Treatment	26	11.3	4.1	5.9	6.4	−1.32

Study 2:

 ...26 girls and 23 boys were recruited from a community-based, after-school program [to be in the treatment group]. A control group (*n* = 41) from a similar after-school program that did not yet incorporate physical activity programming was added.

 The control group concentrated mostly on homework completion, reading, and tutoring.... The physical activity protocol [for the treatment group] included 3 days/week of cardiovascular activities in the form of noncompetitive tasks and games, which alternated among low, medium, and high intensity...over a 12-week period.

 Depression and overall negative mood were assessed on the Profile of Mood States–Short Form...scales of Depression (5 items) and Total mood disturbance (30 items).

Table 2
Depression and Total Mood Disturbance Scores at Weeks 1 and 12 by Group

Profile of Mood States Scale	Week 1		Week 12		*d*
	M	*SD*	*M*	*SD*	
Control (*n* = 41)					
Depression	3.7	3.5	3.8	3.6	.03
Total mood disturbance	16.0	15.8	15.2	15.4	−.05
Treatment (*n* = 49)					
Depression	4.3	3.6	2.4	2.9	−.53
Total mood disturbance	16.8	16.2	11.1	10.9	−.35

[1] Source: Study 1: Annesi, J. J. (2005). Changes in depressed mood associated with 10 weeks of moderate cardiovascular exercise in formerly sedentary adults. *Psychological Reports*, *96*, 855–862. Copyright © 2005 by Psychological Reports. Reprinted with permission. Study 2: Annesi, J. J. (2005). Correlations of depression and total mood disturbance with physical activity and self-concept in preadolescents enrolled in an after-school exercise program. *Psychological Reports*, *96*, 891–898. Copyright © 2005 by Psychological Reports. Reprinted with permission.

Questions for Exercise 21

Part A: Factual Questions

1. At the beginning of Study 1, which group ("treatment group" *or* "control group") had a higher mean depression score?

2. At the end of Study 1, which group ("treatment group" *or* "control group") had a higher mean depression score?

3. In Study 1, which group had a lower mean depression score at Week 10 than at Week 1?

4. In Study 1, the value of *d* for the treatment group is negative. What does the negative indicate?

5. For the treatment group in Study 1, the mean Week 10 depression score was how many standard deviation units different from the mean Week 1 depression score?

6. In Study 1, would it be appropriate to label either of the two effect sizes as "large"? If yes, for which group(s) is it large? Explain.

7. In Study 2, would it be appropriate to label any of the four effect sizes as "large"? If yes, for which group(s) is it large? Explain.

8. In Study 2, would it be appropriate to label any of the four effect sizes as "moderate"? If yes, for which group(s) is it moderate? Explain.

9. In Study 2, would it be appropriate to label any of the four effect sizes as "trivial"? If yes, for which group(s) is it trivial? Explain.

10. Even though it is becoming increasingly common to report effect sizes for the difference between means, many researchers still do not report them. To help in the interpretation of the differences between means, you can usually compute the values of *d* from the statistics that are given. To practice doing this, check the value of *d* for the Depression scores for the treatment group in Study 2 by following Steps A, B, and C:

   A. Subtract the Week 1 mean from the Week 12 mean. What value do you get?

   B. Divide the difference by the standard deviation of the Week 1 scores. What value do you get?

   C. Does your answer to B equal any of the values in the table? Explain.

Part B: Questions for Discussion

11. Examine the four means for the treatment group in Table 2, which are reproduced below, along with the difference between Week 1 and Week 12, obtained by subtracting the mean at Week 12 from the mean at Week 1. The values of *d* are also shown.

Treatment group	Week 1 mean	Week 12 mean	Difference between means	Effect size (*d*) for the difference
Depression	4.3	2.4	−1.9	−.53
Total mood disturbance	16.8	11.1	−5.7	−.35

   Notice that the difference between the means is larger for Total Mood Disturbance than for Depression. Yet, the effect size is larger for Depression than for Total Mood Disturbance. Does this make sense? Explain.

12. Note that the assignment to treatment and control conditions was *not* done at random. Is this a serious issue? Explain.

13. In light of the sample sizes, how much confidence do you have in the results of this study? Explain.

14. Does the fact that the researcher obtained similar results in two experiments using two very different types of participants increase your confidence in the results? Explain.

Exercise 22 Foster Parent Training

Effect Size (d): II

Statistical Guide

Refer to Exercise 21 for general information on the effect size statistic (d). Exercise 21 illustrates how d is used to interpret the difference between pretest and posttest means. It can also be used to interpret the difference between means for an experimental group (i.e., intervention group) and a control group.

In the excerpt in this exercise, d is referred to as the "standardized mean difference statistic." To determine each value of d in the excerpt below, the researchers subtracted the control group's mean from the intervention group's mean and then divided by the mean standard deviation (i.e., the average deviation of the two groups). The result indicates the number of standard deviation units by which the intervention group's mean exceeds the control group's mean.

Excerpt from the Research Article[1]

The final sample consisted of 74 foster parents.... The foster children of parents in the sample were mostly boys....

Qualified participants were randomly assigned to either an intervention or a control group.... The intervention period...continued for two weeks. Parents in the intervention group received the *Anger Outbursts* DVD and were instructed to view the training materials as least once a week. Parents in the control group received no materials during this time.

The Parent Knowledge questionnaire included 20 multiple-choice and true–false items based on content from all segments in the *Anger Outbursts* program.... Scores were reported as the percentage of items correct out of 20. High scores on this measure indicated greater knowledge about anger issues in children.

The Parent Perception questionnaire included [a measure of] *parents' confidence* in having the relevant parenting skills (three items, for example, "I can recognize the different types of anger outbursts in children"). Parents rated on a four-point scale (1 = not at all; 2 = a little; 3 = mostly; 4 = very much).... Scores were reported as the average rating over all items.

Posttest means are presented in Table 1.

Table 1
*Mean Performance on Parent Knowledge and Confidence Scales at Posttest for the National
Sample of Foster Parents*

	Intervention			Control		
	M	*SD*	*n*	*M*	*SD*	*n*
Parent knowledge[a]	71.32	12.39	34	61.38	9.41	40
Parent confidence[b]	2.99	0.42	34	2.84	0.49	40

[a]Standardized mean difference statistic (d) = 0.91.
[b]d = 0.33.

[1] Source: Pacifici, C., Delaney, R., White, L., Cummings, K., & Nelson, C. (2005). Foster parent college: Interactive multimedia training for foster parents. *Social Work Research, 29*, 243–250. Copyright © 2005 by the National Association of Social Workers. Reprinted with permission.

Questions for Exercise 22

Part A: Factual Questions

1. The average intervention group parent answered what percentage of the knowledge questions correctly on the posttest (i.e., what is the mean percentage)?

2. The average control group parent answered what percentage of the knowledge questions correctly on the posttest (i.e., what is the mean percentage)?

3. What is the value of *d* for the difference between your answers to Questions 1 and 2?

4. According to the Statistical Guide in Exercise 21, the effect size in your answer to Question 3 should be labeled as "small." Is this statement "true" *or* "false"? Explain your answer.

5. The mean "Parent confidence" score for the intervention group exceeds the mean "Parent confidence" score for the control group by how many points?

6. What is the value of *d* for the difference in your answer to Question 5? (Hint: The average standard deviation equals $0.42 + 0.49 = 0.91 \div 2 = 0.455$.)

7. According to the Statistical Guide in Exercise 21, the effect size in your answer to Question 6 should be labeled as "small." Is this statement "true" *or* "false"? Explain your answer.

8. Even though it is becoming increasingly common to report effect sizes for the difference between means, many researchers still do not report them. To help in the interpretation of the differences between means, you can usually compute the values of *d* from the statistics that are given. To practice doing this, check the value of *d* for the "Parent knowledge" means by following Steps A, B, C, and D:

    A. Subtract the control group's "Parent knowledge" mean from the intervention group's Parent Knowledge mean. What value do you get?

    B. Compute the mean of the two standard deviations for Parent Knowledge (i.e., sum them and divide by 2). What value do you get?

C. Divide your answer to Step A by your answer to Step B. What value do you get?

D. Does your answer to Step C equal the value in the footnote in the table?

Part B: Questions for Discussion

9. The difference between the mean on Parent Confidence for the intervention group ($m = 2.99$) and the mean for the control group ($m = 2.84$) is small in absolute terms (considerably less than one point). Yet, the effect size is moderate. Speculate on why this is the case.

10. The foster parents were assigned *at random* to the two groups. Is this an important strength of the study? Explain.

Exercise 23   Measuring Functional Abilities of the Elderly
Scattergram

Statistical Guide

A scattergram (also known as a scatterplot or scatter diagram) depicts the relationship between two variables. For each case or participant, one dot is placed to show where the case stands on both variables. Patterns of dots from the lower left to the upper right indicate a direct relationship; patterns from the upper left to the lower right indicate an inverse relationship. The more scatter among the dots, the weaker the relationship.

Note that the horizontal axis in a scattergram is the *x*-axis, while the vertical axis is the *y*-axis.

Excerpt from the Research Article[1]

Performance-based measures of function [in elderly people], particularly activities of daily living…when collected in a standardized clinic setting, are presumed to be a meaningful reflection of the conduct of similar tasks as usually performed in the home. However, the extent to which performance on tasks conducted in a clinic setting under "idealized" conditions of lighting and clinic staff support reflects performance on the same task in the home…is not known.

The 97 participants were 67% female, 24% Black, and 60% aged 65–74…. A total of 20% of the participants in the sample had usual vision worse than 20/40. Between 95% and 100% of participants attempted each task in the home, except for the task of stair climbing, where 56 participants (58%) had no home staircase.

Tests:

Stair climb and descend. The number of seconds to climb up a set of stairs and the time to descend the same set of steps at a lighting level used routinely by the participant. In the clinic, participants are asked to climb seven steps set at a 32-degree incline. Data are presented as number of steps per second.

Plug insertion. The number of seconds to insert a plug into an electrical socket. A socket in the kitchen, preferably at waist level or higher, was selected. In the clinic, a board with a plug and socket is presented at eye level to a participant seated at a desk.

Telephone number look-up and dial. The participant was tested for the number of seconds to locate a telephone number on a standard page in a telephone book. A photocopied page of the local directory and the same number for all participants were used in the clinic setting. The number of seconds required to dial the number on a push-button phone…was recorded.

---

[1] Source: West, S. K., Rubin, G. S., Munoz, B., Abraham, D., & Fried, L. P. (1997). Assessing functional status: Correlation between performance on tasks conducted in a clinic setting and performance on the same task conducted at home. *Journal of Gerontology: Medical Sciences, 52A*, 4, M209–M217. Copyright © by the Gerontology Society of America. Reprinted with permission.

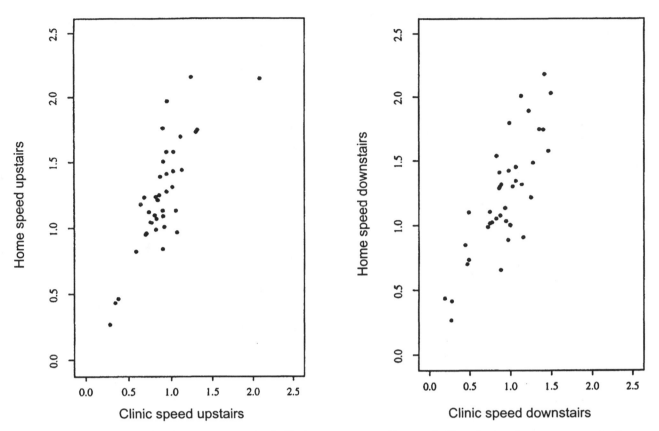

Figure 2. Correlation between speed of climbing upstairs in the clinic versus in the home setting. (Data are in stairs per sec.)

Figure 3. Correlation between speed of climbing downstairs in the clinic versus in the home setting. (Data are in stairs per sec.)

Questions for Exercise 23

Part A: Factual Questions

1. Are the four relationships depicted by the scattergrams "direct" *or* "inverse"? Explain.

2. Examine Figure 3 and find the participant with the best speed in the home. This person descended about how many stairs per second in the home?

3. Did the participant identified in Question 2 have the best performance when tested in the clinic? Explain.

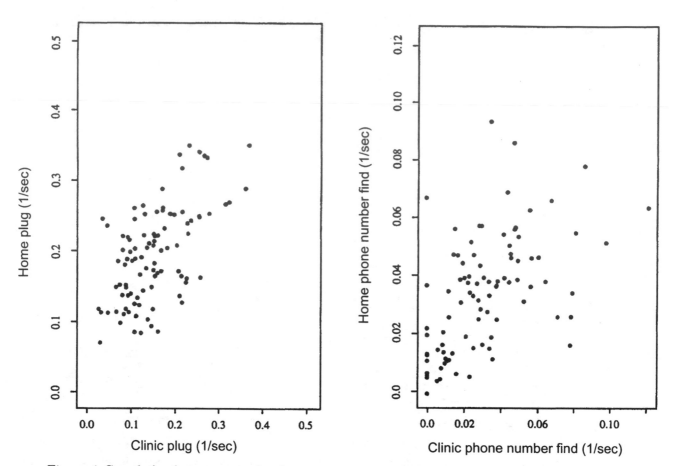

Figure 4. Correlation between speed to insert a plug in a socket in the clinic versus in the home setting. (Data are 1/sec.)

Figure 5. Correlation between speed to find a telephone number in the clinic versus in the home setting. (Data are 1/sec.)

4. Which one of the four scattergrams indicates the strongest relationship?

5. Which one of the four scattergrams indicates the weakest relationship?

6. Is Figure 3 *or* Figure 4 based on a larger number of participants? Explain.

7. The scores obtained in the clinic are listed on which axis in the scattergrams?
    A. The *x*-axis.   B. The *y*-axis.

8. In Figure 2, the person who had a clinic score of about 0.3 (the dot closest to the lower left-hand corner) had about what score when tested at home?

9. In Figure 2, the person who had a clinic score of about 2.2 (the dot closest to the upper right-hand corner) had about what score when tested at home?

Part B: Questions for Discussion

10. Compare your answers to Questions 8 and 9. Do they suggest a direct relationship between the clinic scores and home scores for speed going upstairs? Explain.

11. Suppose you were assessing some elderly people for an important decision such as whether their functioning is adequate for them to continue to live at home without assistance. In your opinion, are the relationships in the figures strong enough to suggest that testing in a clinic alone would yield valid predictions of how well they function at home? (In other words, would it be sufficient to test them only in the clinic in order to make a decision about whether they can function adequately in the home?) Explain.

12. Many textbook authors suggest that the two axes for a scattergram should be about equal in length. The graphic artist who drew the scattergrams in the excerpt failed to follow this suggestion. That is, he or she made the *x*-axis shorter than the *y*-axis in each scattergram. In your opinion, is this failure important? Explain.

13. Are you surprised that the relationships in this excerpt are direct (i.e., positive)? Explain.

Exercise 24   Child Poverty and Mortality

Scattergram and Regression Line

Statistical Guide

See the statistical guide for Exercise 23 to review scattergrams. See the statistical guide for Exercise 6 to review the alternatives to percentages and proportions, in particular, the rate per 100,000.

A regression line drawn through a scattergram shows the overall pattern using a single straight line. The best line for showing this pattern is mathematically calculated. When the line rises from the lower left to the upper right, it indicates that the relationship is direct (i.e., positive). When the line declines from the upper left to the lower right, it indicates that the relationship is inverse (i.e., negative). If the dots on the scattergram all fall exactly on a regression line, the relationship is perfect. The more scattered the dots are around the line, the weaker the relationship. Scattered dots indicate exceptions to the trend indicated by the regression line.

Note that the "participants" in this study are states within the United States.

Excerpt from the Research Article[1]

The federal poverty line, an absolute measure of childhood deprivation that provides a common standard for all U.S. children, was…designed to represent roughly 3 times the average cost of the least expensive nutritionally adequate food plan, as determined by the Department of Agriculture.

…we obtained estimates of the percentage of children living below the federal poverty level in each state from the…poverty estimate files prepared by the U.S. Bureau of the Census [and examined their relationship with child mortality rates].

Questions for Exercise 24

Part A: Factual Questions

1. Compared with other states, does New Hampshire (i.e., NH) have a high *or* low federally referenced child poverty rate? Explain.

2. Compared with other states, is New Hampshire near the top *or* near the bottom in its child mortality rate? Explain.

---

[1] Source: Hillemeier, M. M., Lynch, J., Harper, S., Raghunathan, T., & Kaplan, G. A. (2003). Relative or absolute standards for child poverty: A state-level analysis of infant and child mortality. *American Journal of Public Health, 93*, 652–657. Copyright © 2003 by the American Public Health Association. Reprinted with permission.

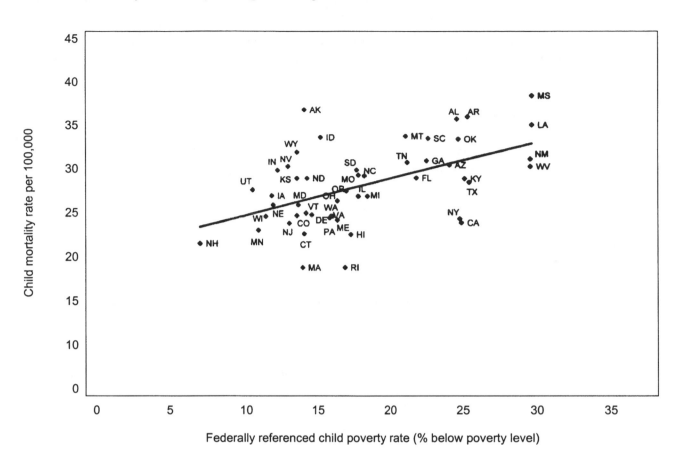

Figure 1. Association between child mortality rates and federally referenced child poverty rates.

3. Do states with high poverty rates also have high mortality rates? If yes, give an example.

4. Do states with low poverty rates also have low mortality rates? If yes, give an example.

5. Considering your answers to Questions 3 and 4, does the relationship seem to be direct (i.e., positive) *or* inverse (i.e., negative)? Explain.

6. Rhode Island (RI) has one of the lowest child mortality rates. Does it also have one of the lowest poverty rates? Explain.

7. Consider the four states at the far right of the scattergram (i.e., MS, LA, NM, and WV). In terms of child mortality rates, a child would have a better chance of surviving childhood in which of these four states?

8. Is Alaska (AK) a good example of a state conforming to the overall trend indicated by the regression line *or* is it an exception? Explain.

9. New Hampshire has a child mortality rate of about 20 per 100,000. Is this mortality rate more *or* is it less than 1%? Explain.

Part B: Questions for Discussion

10. If you were describing the results of this study to another student, would you describe the relationship as being "very strong"? Explain.

11. The poverty rate is defined in terms of the cost of providing a nutritionally adequate food plan. In light of this, does the scattergram indicate that inadequate food plans *cause* childhood mortality? Explain.

12. There is considerable variation from state to state in child poverty rates, from about 8% for NH to about 30% for MS, LA, NM, and WV. Does this amount of variation surprise you? Explain.

13. Based on the data reported in this study, do you agree with this conclusion that the researchers stated as the last sentence of their research report? "In view of the association demonstrated here between child deprivation levels and mortality risk, failure to identify and ameliorate conditions in which families possess inadequate resources may have serious consequences for children's health and for their life chances."

Exercise 25   Community Violence and Achievement

Correlation Coefficient: I

Statistical Guide

A correlation coefficient indicates the strength and direction of a relationship between two variables. The most widely used correlation coefficient is the Pearson r. When it is positive in value, the relationship is direct (i.e., those with high scores on one variable tend to have high scores on the other variable *and* those with low scores on one variable tend to have low scores on the other). In a direct relationship, the closer r is to 1.00, the stronger the relationship; the closer it is to 0.00, the weaker the relationship.

When the value of the Pearson r is negative, the relationship is inverse (i.e., those with high scores on one variable tend to have low scores on the other one). In an inverse relationship, the closer r is to –1.00, the stronger the relationship; the closer it is to 0.00, the weaker the relationship.

Note that in the excerpt, SAT–9 stands for the Ninth Edition of the Stanford Achievement Test, a standardized test that is widely used nationally.

The title of the table in the excerpt refers to "bivariate correlations." The prefix "bi-" means "two." Hence, "bivariate" refers to the fact that there are two variables underlying each correlation coefficient in the table. To read the table, pay attention to the variable numbers, which are in bold.

Excerpt from the Research Article[1]

Participants were recruited from an elementary school located in an urban section of Los Angeles County.... The families living in the surrounding neighborhoods have been conceptualized as "working poor" in recent demographic studies of the Los Angeles region.... All children in 16 third-, fourth-, and fifth-grade classrooms from the participating school were invited to take part in the project. Of these children, 80% returned positive parental permission and assented to participate.

Children completed the Community Experiences Questionnaire.... Items on this measure range in severity from threats to shootings; the 4-point scale ranges from 1 (*never*) to 4 (*a lot of times*).

[An inventory] contained four items assessing bullying by peers ("kids who get hit or pushed by other kids," "kids who get bullied or picked on by other kids," "kids who have mean things said about them by other kids," and "kids who get left out of fun games or play when other kids are trying to hurt their feelings")....

Table 1
Bivariate Correlations Among All Variables

Variable	1	2	3	4	5
Violence exposure					
1. Community violence exposure	—	.20	–.24	–.14	–.26
2. Bullying by peers		—	–.19	–.07	–.25
Academic functioning					
3. SAT–9 Mathematics			—	.60	.64
4. SAT–9 Reading				—	.49
5. GPA					—

[1] Source: Schwartz, D., & Gorman, A. H. (2003). Community violence exposure and children's academic functioning. *Journal of Educational Psychology*, 95, 163–173. Copyright © 2003 by the American Psychological Association, Inc. Reprinted with permission.

Questions for Exercise 25

Part A: Factual Questions

1. What is the value of the correlation for the relationship between variable **1** and variable **2**? (Hint: Find where the row for variable **1** meets the column for variable **2**.)

2. What is the value of the correlation coefficient for the relationship between "SAT–9 Mathematics" and "SAT–9 Reading"?

3. How many of the 10 relationships in the table are inverse?

4. What is the value of the correlation coefficient for the strongest relationship in the table?

5. Which one of the following pairs of variables has a stronger relationship between them?
    A. "Community violence exposure" and "Bullying by peers"
    B. "Community violence exposure" and "SAT–9 Mathematics"

6. Which one of the following pairs of variables has a weaker relationship between them?
    A. "SAT–9 Mathematics" and "SAT–9 Reading"
    B. "SAT–9 Mathematics" and "GPA"

7. The correlation coefficient for the relationship between "Bullying by peers" and "GPA" indicates which of the following?
    A. Those who experience more "Bullying by peers" tend to have higher "GPAs".
    B. Those who experience more "Bullying by peers" tend to have lower "GPAs".

8. The correlation coefficient for the relationship between "SAT–9 Mathematics" and "SAT–9 Reading" indicates which of the following?
    A. Those who are higher in mathematics tend to be higher in reading.
    B. Those who are higher in mathematics tend to be lower in reading.

9. The weakest relationship is between which two variables?

Part B: Questions for Discussion

10. Are you surprised that the relationship between "Bullying by peers" and "GPA" is inverse? Explain.

11. Are you surprised that the relationship between mathematics and reading is direct? Explain.

12. In your opinion, does the Pearson r of $-.26$ prove that being exposed to community violence *causes* lower GPAs?

Exercise 26   Relationships Among Social Variables

Correlation Coefficient: II

Statistical Guide

To review the meaning of the correlation coefficient, see the statistical guide for Exercise 25.

Background Notes

Aggression and withdrawal were measured by showing a picture of all classmates and asking each student to choose two classmates who best fit each descriptor. For *aggression*, a score was obtained for each child by summing the number of times he or she was selected for these descriptors: "gets into lots of fights," "loses temper easily," "too bossy," and "picks on other kids." For *withdrawal*, a score was obtained for each child by summing the number of times he or she was selected for these descriptors: "rather play alone than with others" and "very shy."

Social preference was assessed by asking each child to name three other children they would like most and like least for playing together, inviting others to a birthday party, and sitting next to each other on a bus. [Responses were scored in such a way that higher scores indicate greater social preference.]

Victimization by peers was measured by asking each child to nominate up to five other students who could be described as being made fun of, being called names, and getting hit and pushed by other kids. [Higher scores indicate greater victimization.]

Number of affiliative links was measured by asking, "You have probably noticed children in your class who often hang around together and others who are more often alone. Could you name the children who often hang around together?" [Higher scores indicate a larger number of affiliative links.]

Loneliness was measured with a 16-item questionnaire with higher scores indicating greater loneliness.

Perceived social acceptance and *behavior-conflict* were two aspects of self-concept measured with Harter's Self-Perception Profile for Children, which is a questionnaire. Higher scores reflect a better self-concept in each of the two domains.

Excerpt from the Research Article[1]

French Canadian children (393 girls, 400 boys; mean age = 115 months, range 8 to 10 years) participated in the study. The children attended third ($n = 315$), fourth ($n = 248$), and fifth ($n = 230$) grades in 10 elementary schools from a variety of socioeconomic backgrounds....

Table 1 presents the correlations among the measures considered in the present study.

---

[1] Source: Boivin, M., & Hymel, S. (1997). Peer experiences and social self-perceptions: A sequential model. *Developmental Psychology*, 33, 135–143. Copyright © 1997 by the American Psychological Association, Inc. Reprinted with permission.

Table 1
Correlations Among the Social Behavior, Peer Experiences, and Self-Perception Measures

Measure	1	2	3	4	5	6	7	8
1. Withdrawal	—							
2. Aggression	−.10	—						
3. Social preference	−.39	−.44	—					
4. Victimization by peers	.42	.53	−.68	—				
5. No. of affiliative links	−.35	.05	.35	−.21	—			
6. Loneliness	.29	.12	−.34	.34	−.18	—		
7. Perceived social acceptance	−.27	−.04	.28	−.26	.18	−.69	—	
8. Perceived behavior–conflict	.06	−.32	.17	−.17	−.06	−.35	.39	—

Questions for Exercise 26

Part A: Factual Questions

1. What is the value of the Pearson *r* for the relationship between "Withdrawal" and "Aggression"?

2. What is the value of the Pearson *r* for the relationship between "Loneliness" and "Perceived social acceptance"?

3. Is the relationship between "Withdrawal" and "Loneliness" direct *or* inverse? Explain the basis for your answer.

4. Is the relationship between "Loneliness" and "Social preference" direct *or* inverse? Explain the basis for your answer.

5. Which variable has the strongest relationship with "Withdrawal"? Explain.

6. Which variable has the weakest relationship with "Withdrawal"? Explain.

7. The Pearson *r* for the relationship between "Withdrawal" and "Loneliness" indicates that those who tend to be more lonely tend to be

    A. more withdrawn.   B. less withdrawn.

8. Which of the following pairs of variables has the strongest relationship between them?

   A. "Perceived social acceptance" and "Loneliness"
   B. "Withdrawal" and "Victimization by peers"
   C. "No. of affiliative links" and "Aggression"

9. Which of the following pairs of variables has the weakest relationship between them?

   A. "Withdrawal" and "Social preference"
   B. "Withdrawal" and "Perceived social acceptance"
   C. "Withdrawal" and "Perceived behavior–conflict"

Part B: Questions for Discussion

10. In words (without using numbers), how would you describe the strength and direction of the relationship between "Withdrawal" and "Aggression"?

11. In words (without using numbers), how would you describe the strength and direction of the relationship between "Victimization by peers" and "Social preference"?

12. In your opinion, does it make sense that the Pearson r for the relationship between "Loneliness" and "Perceived social acceptance" is −.69? Explain.

13. In your opinion, does the Pearson r of −.27 for the relationship between "Withdrawal" and "Perceived social acceptance" prove that being withdrawn *causes* less perceived social acceptance? Explain.

Exercise 27   Commitment and Job Performance

Meta-Analysis with Correlation Coefficients

Statistical Guide

To review the correlation coefficient, see the statistical guide for Exercise 25.

In a meta-analysis, results from previous studies (usually conducted by a variety of researchers who have studied a single topic) are statistically combined in order to arrive at an overall result for all the studies. For instance, in the excerpt below, the mean correlation coefficient for 27 different studies was computed to get an overall estimate of the correlation between organizational commitment and job performance. Typically, in the computation of the mean across studies, researchers "weight" the studies according to sample size. That is, when computing the mean, they give more weight to the results of studies with more participants than to the results of studies with fewer participants.[1]

Excerpt from the Research Article[2]

Our meta-analysis is based on a large sample of 3,630 participants compiled from 27 studies.

Attitudinal commitment is the strength of an employee's emotional attachment to an organization and acceptance of the organization's goals and values....

The sample size weighted mean of the 27 sample correlations [in Table 1] was .14, suggesting a weak positive relationship between organizational commitment and job performance. However, the strength of this relationship may be misleading if employee tenure [defined in various studies as either number of years employed by an organization or number of years in a particular job] is moderating the relationship between organizational commitment and job performance. (See Table 1 on the next page.)

Questions for Exercise 27

Part A: Factual Questions

1. The "Average tenure" in the 27 studies ranged from one-quarter year (i.e., 0.25) to how many years?

2. What was the "Average age" in Study 20 by Steers?

---

[1] If you have taken a course in statistics, you may know that when averaging correlation coefficients, they should first be converted to values of Fisher's Z, which are then averaged. Finally, the average value of Z is then converted back into the average correlation coefficient.

[2] Source: Wright, T. A., & Bonett, D. G. (2002). The moderating effects of employee tenure on the relation between organizational commitment and job performance: A meta-analysis. *Journal of Applied Psychology, 87*, 1183–1190. Copyright © 2002 by the American Psychological Association, Inc. Reprinted with permission.

Table 1

Average Tenure, Average Age, Pearson Correlation, and Sample Size for Each Study Sample

Study	Average tenure (years)	Average age (years)	Pearson r[a]	N
1. Stumpf & Hartman (1984)	0.25	28.4	.62	85
2. Bauer & Green (1998)	0.5	23.5	.45	112
3. Mowday et al. (1979)	0.5	25.0	.35	59
4. Adkins (1995)	0.5	—	.34	171
5. Saks (1996)	1.0	23.8	.26	55
6. Van Maanen (1975)	2.5	26.5	.26	36
7. DeCotiis & Summers (1987)	2.7	28.6	.12	89
8. M. L. Williams, Podsakoff, & Huber (1992)	3.4	37.8	.16	300
9. Shore & Martin (1989)	3.4	36.7	.03	69
10. Cropanzano et al. (1993)	3.6	—	.33	35
11. Cropanzano et al. (1993)	4.0	30.5	.28	138
12. L. J. Williams & Anderson (1991)	4.0	30.0	.05	127
13. Shore & Martin (1989)	4.3	35.5	.05	68
14. Somers & Birnbaum (1998)	4.7	35.6	.12	109
15. D. M. Randall, Fedor, & Longenecker (1990)	5.0	39.0	.24	156
16. Settoon, Bennett, & Liden (1996)	5.7	34.7	.01	102
17. Jamal (1984)	6.0	31.0	.07	440
18. Meyer et al. (1989)	6.0	36.7	.19	61
19. Hackett et al. (1994)	7.9	40.7	.00	80
20. Steers (1977)	8.0	35.0	.05	382
21. T. W. Lee & Mowday (1987)	8.0	38.1	.09	445
22. O'Reilly & Chatman (1986)	9.0	—	.10	82
23. Steers (1977)	10.0	38.0	.05	119
24. Wiener & Vardi (1980)	—	42.0	.15	56
25. Angle & Lawson (1994)	—	43.0	.04	85
26. M. L. Randall, Cropanzano, Bormann, & Birjulin (1999)	10.4	41.0	.17	128
27. Wright (1997)	16.5	46.1	−.26	41

Note. Dashes indicate data that were not reported in original study.

[a]Pearson correlation between commitment and job performance.

3. How many of the values of Pearson r are greater than .50?

4. How many of the values of Pearson r are greater than .30?

5. Which of the 27 studies was given the greatest weight in calculating the mean?

6. The correlation coefficient for Study 1 by Stumpf & Hartman indicates which of the following?

  A. Those who are higher in commitment tend to be higher in job performance.
  B. Those who are higher in commitment tend to be lower in job performance.
  C. There is no relationship between commitment and job performance.

7. The correlation coefficient for Study 27 by Wright indicates which of the following?

  A. Those who are higher in commitment tend to be higher in job performance.
  B. Those who are higher in commitment tend to be lower in job performance.
  C. There is no relationship between commitment and job performance.

8. The correlation coefficient for Study 19 by Hackett et al. indicates which of the following?

  A. Those who are higher in commitment tend to be higher in job performance.
  B. Those who are higher in commitment tend to be lower in job performance.
  C. There is no relationship between commitment and job performance.

9. In general, which of the following is true?

  A. Studies in which the average tenure is low tend to have higher correlations.
  B. Studies in which the average tenure is low tend to have lower correlations.

Part B: Questions for Discussion

10. Based on what you know about the Pearson r, do you agree with the researchers' interpretation that a correlation of .14 represents a "weak positive relationship"?

11. Based on your reading of research in the social and behavioral sciences, do you agree with the authors that 3,630 participants constitute a "large sample"?

12. Does it surprise you that those with more tenure tend to be older? Explain.

Exercise 28   Alcohol Consumption and Related Variables

Correlation Coefficient and Coefficient of Determination: I

Statistical Guide

To review correlation coefficients, see the statistical guide for Exercise 25.

The coefficient of determination is r squared; its symbol is r^2. For instance, if $r = .50$, then, $r^2 = .50 \times .50 = .25$. Multiplying this result by 100 yields the *explained variance* (also known as the amount of *variance accounted for*) expressed as a percentage. In this example, the explained variance expressed as a percentage is $.25 \times 100 = 25\%$. This indicates that a Pearson r of .50 represents a relationship that is 25% higher than a Pearson r of 0.00 (that is, it is 25% better than no relationship). It is important to notice that a Pearson r of .50 is *not* 50%. The coefficient of determination must be used to determine the correct percentage for interpreting the value of Pearson r.

The interpretation of a coefficient of determination for a negative value of r is the same as for a positive value except that it applies to an *inverse* relationship. For instance, .16 (a positive value) is the coefficient of determination for an r of $-.40$ (a negative value). Multiplying by 100, we learn that a value of $-.40$ is 16% away from 0.00 *in the negative direction*. Coefficients of determination are always positive because of the squaring. Hence, we use positive values of the coefficient of determination to interpret both positive and negative values of r.

Excerpt from the Research Article[1]

Participants were 23 older adults (16 men and 7 women).… The majority of these individuals were in high-level corporate management positions.

The CES-D is a 20-item questionnaire designed to measure levels of depression.…

The Fat Intake Scale (FIS) is a brief dietary questionnaire.…

Alcohol consumption. Alcohol consumption for each participant was computed by multiplying quantity (drinks per occasion) by frequency (drinking days per week). Self-reported levels of tension/anxiety were significantly negatively correlated with alcohol consumption ($r = -.45$), suggesting an inverse relationship between tension/anxiety and alcohol consumption. Neither depression nor any of the anger scores were correlated with alcohol consumption.

Saturated fat intake. Scores on the CES-D correlated with scores on the FIS ($r = .68$), suggesting a direct and positive relationship between level of depression and saturated fat intake. Scores on the Trait-Anger scale and the Anger Expression scale were also correlated with the FIS ($r = .51$ and .52, respectively), also suggesting a direct and positive relationship between level of trait anger and external anger expression with saturated fat intake.

Exercise: Aerobic and strength training. Scores on the Trait-Anger scale were significantly negatively correlated with the self-reported level of aerobic exercise ($r = -.44$), suggesting an inverse relationship between level of trait anger and level of aerobic exercise. Scores on Anger Expression were, however, positively correlated with self-reported level of strength training ($r = .51$), suggesting a strong positive relationship between level of internal anger expression and engagement in strength training.

---

[1] Source: Anton, S. D., & Miller, P. M. (2005). Do negative emotions predict alcohol consumption, saturated fat intake, and physical activity in older adults? *Behavior Modification*, *29*, 677–688. Copyright © 2005 by Sage Publications. Reprinted with permission.

Questions for Exercise 28

Part A: Factual Questions

1. Is the relationship between levels of tension/anxiety and alcohol consumption "direct" *or* "inverse"? (*Note to instructors*: All the reported correlation coefficients in the excerpt are statistically significant at the .05 or higher levels.)

2. The Pearson *r* for the relationship between CES-D depression scores and FIS fat intake scores indicates that

   A. higher depression is associated with less fat intake.
   B. higher depression is associated with more fat intake.

3. What is the value of the coefficient of determination for the relationship between "tension/anxiety" and "alcohol consumption"? Explain how you computed the answer.

4. What is the value of the coefficient of determination for the relationship between CES–D scores and FIS scores? Explain how you computed the answer.

5. What is the value of the coefficient of determination for the relationship between Anger Expression scores and levels of strength training scores? Explain how you computed the answer.

6. The correlation coefficient for the relationship between Anger Expression scores and FIS scores is .52. What percentage of the variance for Anger Expression is explained by the variance for FIS? Explain how you computed the answer.

7. What percentage of the variance for alcohol consumption is predicted by the variance for tension/anxiety? Explain how you computed the answer.

8. In the excerpt, six correlation coefficients are reported. For which correlation coefficient is the associated coefficient of determination highest?

9. In the excerpt, six correlation coefficients are reported. For which correlation coefficient is the associated coefficient of determination lowest?

Part B: Questions for Discussion

10. Does it surprise you that there is a direct relationship between depression and fat intake? Explain.

11. Consider the correlation coefficient of .68 for the relationship between CES-D and FIS. Would you characterize the relationship as being "strong"? Explain.

12. Consider the correlation coefficient of .68 for the relationship between CES-D and FIS. Then, consider the corresponding percentage of explained variance. Does consideration of the percentage of explained variance influence your impression of the strength of the relationship? Explain.

Exercise 29   New Parents Project

Correlation Coefficient and Coefficient of Determination: II

Statistical Guide

To review correlation coefficients, see the statistical guide for Exercise 25. To review coefficients of determination and percentage of explained variance, see the statistical guide for Exercise 28.

Excerpt from the Research Article[1]

The 21 adolescent mothers were between the ages of 16 and 19 years.... [They had been recruited by Parents Project] personnel and then contacted by one of the researchers to solicit their participation. [The instruments that were used were]:

Revised UCLA Loneliness Scale.... Scores range from 20 to 80; the higher the score, the greater the loneliness.

Rosenberg Self-Esteem Scale. Self-esteem was measured using the 10-item...scale. Positively and negatively worded items were included in the scale to reduce the likelihood of response set. When five items are reverse-scored, higher scores indicate greater self-esteem.

Social Support Questionnaire—Short Form. Respondents list the people they can rely on for support in a given set of circumstances and indicate overall level of satisfaction with the support provided.

Center for Epidemiologic Studies Depression Scale for Children [CES-DC; with 20 items]. Scores higher than 15 indicate the presence of depressive symptomatology.

There was a negative relationship between depression and social support ($r = -.61$). Social support was positively associated with self-esteem ($r = .65$) and negatively associated with loneliness ($r = -.50$). Loneliness was correlated with depression ($r = .53$) and inversely correlated with self-esteem ($r = -.74$).

Questions for Exercise 29

Part A: Factual Questions

1. Which value of r in the excerpt represents the strongest relationship?

2. Those who are high on "depression" tend to have what type of score on "social support"?

   A. A relatively high score
   B. A relatively low score

---

[1] Source: Hudson, D. B., Elek, S. M., & Campbell-Grossman, C. (2000). Depression, self-esteem, loneliness, and social support among adolescent mothers participating in the new parents project. *Adolescence, 335,* 445–453. Copyright © 2000 by Libra Publishers, Inc. Reprinted with permission.

3. Those who are high on "self-esteem" tend to have what type of score on "social support"?

    A. A relatively high score
    B. A relatively low score

4. Which of the five correlation coefficients given in the excerpt has the smallest coefficient of determination? (Try to answer this question without performing any computations.)

5. To two decimal places, what is the value of the coefficient of determination for the correlation you referred to in your answer to Question 4?

6. What is the percentage of explained variance (variance accounted for) that corresponds to your answer to Question 5?

7. To two decimal places, what is the value of the coefficient of determination for the relationship between "loneliness" and "self-esteem"?

8. What is the percentage of explained variance (variance accounted for) that corresponds to your answer to Question 7?

9. For the relationship between "depression" and "social support," what is the percentage of variance accounted for?

Part B: Questions for Discussion

10. Would you characterize any of the relationships in the excerpt as being "strong"? Explain.

11. Before this study was conducted, would you have hypothesized that the relationship between "loneliness" and "depression" would be direct *or* inverse? Explain.

12. Would you be willing to generalize the results of this study to all adolescent mothers in the country? Explain.

Exercise 30   Reliability of a Rating Scale

Test–Retest Reliability Coefficient and Coefficient of Determination

Statistical Guide

To review correlation coefficients, see the statistical guide for Exercise 25. To review coefficients of determination and percentage of explained variance, see the statistical guide for Exercise 28.

To determine test–retest reliability, a test is administered to one group of examinees twice (often with a week or two intervening between the two administrations of the test). This yields two scores for each examinee. Computing a correlation coefficient for the relationship between the two sets of scores indicates the stability of the scores over time. For instance, a high correlation coefficient indicates that those who scored high on the first administration also scored high on the second administration; likewise, those who scored low on the first administration also scored low on the second administration.

When a *correlation coefficient* is used to express the stability of test scores over time, the coefficient is commonly referred to as a *test–retest reliability coefficient*. Despite the difference in names, a test–retest reliability coefficient is mathematically the same as a correlation coefficient.

Excerpt from the Research Article[1]

We assessed the reliability of the Behavioral and Emotional Rating Scale—Second Edition; Parent Rating Scale (BERS–2; PRS).

All parents of kindergarteners through second graders at the elementary school ($N = 122$) and sixth graders at the middle school ($N = 169$) received by mail a…copy of the PRS…. Parents were informed that on receipt of the first protocol, a second PRS would be sent to them that was also to be filled out and returned…. A return rate of 26.8 percent was achieved.

Assessments like the PRS, which may be used for screening, planning, and evaluation purposes and for which data are reported individually, should have reliability coefficients of at least .80.

Table 1
Means, Standard Deviations, and Test–Retest Correlations for the BERS-2 Parent Rating Scale

| | Elementary school sample ($N = 33$) | | | | | Middle school sample ($N = 45$) | | | | | Total sample | | | | |
| | First testing | | Second testing | | | First testing | | Second testing | | | First testing | | Second testing | | |
Subscales	M	SD	M	SD	r	M	SD	M	SD	r	M	SD	M	SD	r
Interpersonal	9.64	3.31	9.18	2.93	.91	10.96	2.82	10.96	2.67	.89	10.40	3.08	10.21	2.90	.89
Family involvement	9.91	2.73	10.06	2.68	.94	10.91	2.83	10.91	2.76	.92	10.49	2.81	10.55	2.74	.93
Intrapersonal	10.39	3.11	10.27	2.93	.93	10.04	3.16	11.11	2.90	.88	10.77	3.14	10.76	2.92	.90
School functioning	9.76	3.12	9.30	3.12	.86	11.33	2.74	11.49	2.49	.88	10.67	2.99	10.56	2.96	.86
Affective	11.09	2.65	10.76	2.70	.90	10.96	2.92	10.98	2.77	.82	11.01	2.79	10.88	2.73	.86
Career	8.69	3.42	8.19	3.67	.80	10.71	2.43	10.55	2.24	.90	9.92	3.01	9.57	3.12	.85
Strength index	100.88	18.31	99.16	17.37	.90	106.80	17.52	107.20	16.30	.87	104.29	19.99	103.79	17.13	.88

Note. Means are reported as standard scores.

[1] Source: Mooney, P., Epstein, M. H., Ryser, G., & Pierce, C. D. (2005). Reliability and validity of the Behavioral and Emotional Rating Scale—Second Edition: Parent Rating Scale. *Children & Schools, 27*, 147–155. Copyright © 2005 by the National Association of Social Workers. Reprinted with permission.

Questions for Exercise 30

Part A: Factual Questions

1. For the elementary school sample, which subscale had the lowest test–retest reliability coefficient?

2. For the middle-school sample, which subscale had the highest test–retest reliability coefficient?

3. For the total sample, what is the value of the test–retest reliability coefficient for "School functioning"?

4. The researchers state that measures used to assess individuals should have test–retest reliability coefficients of at least .80. Do all the subscales meet this criterion?

5. For the total sample, what is the value of the test–retest reliability coefficient for "Family involvement"?

6. What is the value of the coefficient of determination for your answer to Question 5?

7. Based on your answer to Question 6, what percentage of the variance on one administration of the "Family involvement" subscale is explained by the variance on the other administration of the same scale?

8. The researchers state that measures used to assess individuals should have test–retest reliability coefficients of at least .80. For a coefficient of .80, what percentage of the variance on one administration of the "Family involvement" subscale is explained by the variance on the other administration of the same scale?

Part B: Questions for Discussion

9. Consider a college admissions test. In your opinion, how important is it for such a test to have a high test–retest reliability coefficient?

10. The return rate was 26.8%. Does this surprise you?

11. Does the fact that the response rate was considerably less than 100% affect your evaluation of this study? Explain.

Exercise 31   Predictors of Suicidality

Multiple Correlation: I

Statistical Guide

To review correlation coefficients, see the statistical guide for Exercise 25.

A multiple correlation coefficient (R) indicates the extent to which a *combination of variables* predicts an outcome variable. (In the excerpt below, the researchers determine how well a combination of variables predicts suicidality. In this case, the multiple R tells us how well we can predict if we use a *combination* of all the variables in Table 1.)

Squaring R yields the coefficient of determination, whose symbol is R^2. The coefficient of determination is the proportion of variance in the outcome that is predicted by the combination of two or more predictor variables. This proportion is sometimes called the *explained variance* or *variance accounted for*. Multiplying R^2 by 100% yields the percentage of variance accounted for.

Background Notes

In the following excerpt, "CAST" refers to the Children of Alcoholics Screening Test, which was used to measure the extent of parental alcohol problems.

For all variables, higher scores indicate more of the characteristic in question.

Excerpt from the Research Article[1]

Participants in this study ($N = 349$) were young males ($M = 19$ years, $SD = 3.97$, range $= 13$ to 30 years) from a Los Angeles County community sample who were self-identified as Latino.

Behavioral, attitudinal, and cognitive components related to suicidality were assessed with a 6-item scale.... This scale contains [item questions such as] "I have been thinking about ways to kill myself" [and] "I have had recent thoughts about dying...." Responses ranged from 1 (*never*) to 5 (*always*).

(*See Table 1 on the next page.*)

---

[1] Source: Locke, T. F., & Newcomb, M. D. (2005). Psychosocial predictors and correlates of suicidality in teenage Latino males. *Hispanic Journal of Behavioral Sciences*, *27*, 319–336. Copyright © 2005 by Sage Publications. Reprinted with permission.

Table 1
Correlation and Multiple Regression Results

Variable tested	Correlation with suicidality	Multiple correlation
Sexual abuse	.38	
Emotional abuse	.45	
Physical abuse	.35	
Emotional neglect	.23	
Physical neglect	.31	
CAST—mother	.28	
CAST—father	.23	
Childhood quality	−.24	
Good relationship with parents	−.36	
Good relationship with family	−.27	
Assertiveness	−.13	
Problem-solving confidence	−.21	
Competence	−.24	
Religious commitment	−.18	
Law abiding	−.27	
Cigarette use	.15	
Alcohol use	.15	
Marijuana use	.26	
Hard drug use	.38	
R		.61
R^2		.37

CAST = Children of Alcoholics Screening Test, Short Form.

Questions for Exercise 31

Part A: Factual Questions

1. In Table 1, does "Sexual abuse" *or* "Emotional abuse" correlate more highly with suicidality?

2. The correlation between "Religious commitment" and suicidality indicates which of the following?

   A. Those individuals with more "Religious commitment" report more suicidality.
   B. Those individuals with more "Religious commitment" report less suicidality.

3. The correlation between "Hard drug use" and suicidality indicates which of the following?

   A. Those individuals with more "Hard drug use" report more suicidality.
   B. Those individuals with more "Hard drug use" report less suicidality.

4. Is "Alcohol use" *or* "Childhood quality" a better predictor of suicidality?

5. What is the value of the multiple correlation coefficient when all the predictor variables in Table 1 are used in combination to predict suicidality?

6. What is the value of the coefficient of determination that corresponds to the multiple correlation coefficient?

7. What proportion of the variance in suicidality is predicted by the combination of all the predictors in Table 1?

8. What percentage of the variance in suicidality is predicted by the combination of all the predictors in Table 1?

Part B: Questions for Discussion

9. Does it surprise you that some of the individual predictors of suicidality have positive correlations while others have negative correlations?

10. Based on what you know about the interpretation of correlation coefficients, would you characterize the multiple correlation coefficient in Table 1 as representing a strong relationship? Explain.

Exercise 32   Predicting College GPA

Multiple Correlation: II

Statistical Guide

To review correlation coefficients, see the statistical guide for Exercise 25. To review multiple correlation and the coefficient of determination, see the statistical guide for Exercise 31.

Table 1 shows how well the individual tests predict GPA. Table 2 shows how much R (and the corresponding value of R^2) are increased as additional tests are added into the formula for R.

Excerpt from the Research Article[1]

The D-48, a nonverbal test of general intelligence, is widely used in Europe and other areas of the world but is virtually unknown in the United States. In this study, the D-48 and the School and College Ability Tests (SCAT) [which are widely used in the U.S.] were administered to a sample of 250 community college students.... Of the 250 students, 145 were Mexican American and 105 were Anglo-American. [Means for ethnicity and gender were not significantly different.] A step-wise regression analysis indicated an R^2 of .36 with grade point average (GPA), with the D-48 entered as a second variable behind the SCAT Total.

Table 1
Correlation Coefficients Between D-48, GPA, and SCAT Scores

| | Samples | | | |
| | Mexican American | | Anglo-American | |
	Males	Females	Males	Females
D-48 and GPA	.41	.50	.45	.49
SCAT Total and GPA	.54	.66	.52	.58
SCAT Quantitative and GPA	.56	.51	.53	.46
SCAT Verbal and GPA	.45	.58	.42	.51

Note. The statistics in this table are Pearson rs—not multiple Rs.

Table 2
Results of Step-Wise Multiple Regression

| | Multiple | | |
Variable Entered	R	R^2	Increase in R^2
1. SCAT Total	.537	.288	.288
2. D-48	.583	.340	.052
3. SCAT Quantitative	.598	.358	.018
4. SCAT Verbal	.602	.362	.004

Note. The statistics in this table are based on the total sample of Mexican American and Anglo-American students.

---

[1] Source: Domino, G., & Morales, A. (2000). Reliability and validity of the D-48 with Mexican American college students. *Hispanic Journal of Behavioral Sciences*, *22*, 382–389. Copyright © 2000 by Sage Publications, Inc. Reprinted with permission.

Questions for Exercise 32

Part A: Factual Questions

1. In Table 1, which variable correlates most highly with "GPA" for Mexican American males?

2. In Table 1, which variable is the best predictor of "GPA" for Anglo-American males?

3. In Table 1, which variable is the least predictive of "GPA" for Mexican American females?

4. By how much does R^2 increase when the "D-48" is added to the "SCAT Total"?

5. What is the value of the multiple correlation coefficient when "SCAT Total" and "D-48" are used together?

6. How much of the variance in "GPA" is accounted for by the combination of "SCAT Total" and "D-48"?

7. What is the value of the multiple correlation coefficient when all four variables are used in combination to predict "GPA"?

8. To two decimal places, what is the value of the coefficient of determination that corresponds to your answer to Question 7?

Part B: Questions for Discussion

9. The best predictor of grades (i.e., "GPA") for Mexican American females is "SCAT Total" ($r = .66$). How would you describe the strength of this relationship (e.g., "perfect," "extremely strong," and so on)?

10. In your opinion, is the increase provided by using the "D-48" in conjunction with the "SCAT Total" large enough to justify having students take an additional test?

11. The SCAT is used three times in the multiple regression (as a total score, the verbal score, and the quantitative score). Does it make sense to use all three in such an analysis? Explain.

Exercise 33 Dieting, Age, and Body Fat

Linear Regression

Statistical Guide

To review scattergrams, see the statistical guide for Exercise 23.

In simple linear regression, a single straight line is mathematically fitted to describe the dots on a scattergram. The equation for any straight line is $y = a + bx$, where a is the intercept (i.e., the score value where the line meets the vertical axis) and b is the slope (i.e., the rate of change or the direction and angle of the line). Note that for a direct relationship, the slope will be positive in value; for an inverse relationship, it will be negative. After the best-fitting line has been mathematically determined for a particular scattergram, the values for x (the scores) can be inserted and the formula solved to obtain predicted values on y.

Background Notes

In the study described below, the subjects' body fat was pretested and posttested to assess the effects of a very low calorie diet. Hydrodensitometry measures body fat in water; bioelectrical impedance analysis (BIA) is an electrical measure of body fat.

Excerpt from the Research Article[1]

Seventeen subjects (nine women and eight men) from an outpatient, hospital-based treatment program for obesity volunteered.

Within 10 days after the baseline measures (i.e., pretest measures) were obtained, the subjects began the 12-week VLCD [very low calorie diet] portion of the...program.... At the end of the 12 weeks, all measurements were repeated in the laboratory.

Figure 1 demonstrates the relationship between age and percent of weight loss as fat. The correlation coefficient for this relationship was $r = -.49$.

Correlation between hydrostatic weighing and bioelectrical impedance was $r = .63$ for the 16 pretests and $r = .84$ for the 17 posttests. (Hydrostatic measurement of one male subject was not possible on the pretest because of discomfort in the water.) Correlation for the combined pretest and posttest trials ($n = 33$) was $r = .837$ (Figure 2).

---

[1] Source: Burgess, N. S. (1991). Effect of a very low calorie diet on body composition and resting metabolic rate in obese men and women. *Journal of the American Dietetic Association, 91*, 430–434. Copyright © by The American Dietetic Association. Reprinted with permission.

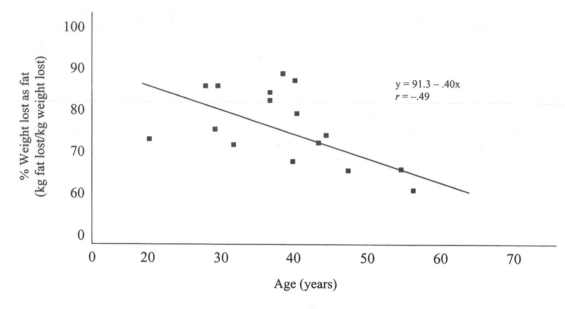

Figure 1. Relationship of age to fat loss.

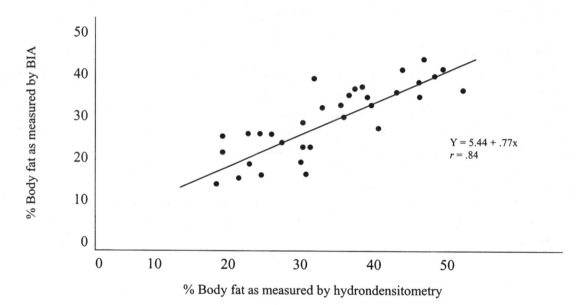

Figure 2. Hydrodensitometry vs. bioelectrical impedance.

Questions for Exercise 33

Part A: Factual Questions

1. Which figure illustrates a direct relationship? Explain.

2. Which figure has a negative slope? Is the corresponding correlation coefficient also negative?

3. If the line in Figure 1 was extended to the left, at what value would it meet the vertical axis (i.e., *y*-axis)? (Give an answer that is precise to one decimal place.)

4. What is the value of the intercept in Figure 2?

5. Is the relationship depicted in Figure 1 *or* Figure 2 stronger? Explain.

6. Use the equation for the straight line shown in Figure 1 to predict the percentage of weight lost as fat for a person who is 60 years of age.

7. Use the equation for the straight line shown in Figure 1 to predict the percentage of weight lost as fat for a person who is 20 years of age.

8. Compare your answers to Questions 6 and 7. Do your answers make sense considering that the relationship is inverse? Explain.

9. Use the equation for the straight line shown in Figure 2 to predict the percentage of body fat as measured by BIA for a person who has 50% body fat as measured by hydrodensitometry.

10. The equation in which figure will yield more accurate predictions? Explain.

Part B: Questions for Discussion

11. Suppose the slope in Figure 2 had been 1.50 instead of 0.77. With a slope of 1.50, would the line rise (from left to right) more steeply or less steeply than the line shown in Figure 2?

12. The correlation coefficient for the relationship between the two methods for measuring body fat is less than perfect. What does this tell us about the two methods of measurement?

13. Speculate on why we use a line based on the entire group to make predictions instead of using the values of individuals to make predictions. (For example, the person who is about 58 years of age in Figure 1 lost about 62% of weight as body fat. In the future, why don't we just predict that all those who are 58 years of age will lose 62% body fat?)

Exercise 34   Excerpts on Sampling

Bias in Sampling

Statistical Guide

In unbiased sampling, each member of a population has an equal chance of being included in a sample. Random sampling is the basic method used to obtain unbiased samples. Self-selection, volunteering, and any other nonrandom event (e.g., choosing people who happen to be convenient to serve as participants in a study) bias a sample. *Do not assume that a sample was drawn at random unless the researcher explicitly states this was done.*

Questions for Exercise 34

Directions: For each of the following excerpts from journal articles, indicate whether the sample is biased or unbiased and explain your choice. In some cases, you may answer "not sure" because there is insufficient information to make a judgment. If you answer "not sure" to an item, describe the additional information you would like to have before making a choice.

1. Researchers state, "To help resolve the questions posed above [in this research report], a telephone survey of 1,000 California residents was conducted...using random digit dialing (RDD). Sampling by means of RDD avoids the threat of systematically excluding that portion of the population with unlisted telephone numbers."[1]

2. Researchers state, "Nine counseling sites were invited to participate in the study. These sites were selected to provide a representative range of the types of locations at which counseling takes place. The locations were a university counseling center, a psychology training clinic, a women's center, a Lutheran Social Service center, two community mental health centers, and three private psychology practices. Two of the private practice sites declined to participate."[2]

3. Researchers state, "33 White (63.6% female) and 18 ethnic minority (61.1% female) Cornell University students participated. Participants were recruited from psychology and human development classes and various other campus locations."[3]

4. Researchers state, "A sample of 60 was randomly selected from 125 people arrested on DWI offenses and referred by the county to a professional evaluator between May 2000 and December 2003."[4]

5. A researcher states, "The participants were 38 early adolescent Latino boys and girls (20 boys, 18 girls). All students in the eighth grade (in this urban school district, most elementary schools included kindergarten through eighth grade) social studies classrooms in two midwestern urban elementary schools were invited to participate in the study. Students had been assigned randomly

to the classrooms. Students who returned parental consent forms (approximately 60% of those invited) were interviewed individually [for this study]....”[5]

6. Researchers state that “Balancing the needs for efficiency and minimizing potential error, we developed a sampling plan to collect data from a representative stratified random sample of the 367 Wisconsin school districts with elementary schools...the stratification characteristic was socioeconomic status represented by the proportion of students eligible for the federal free and reduced-cost lunch program.... Districts were chosen within strata.”[6]

7. Researchers state that “Briefly, a stratified random sample of 4,907 coronary artery disease patients undergoing an angiogram at one...New York State hospital...was selected for the medical records abstraction portion of the study.”[7]

8. Researchers state that “We commissioned Survey Sampling Incorporated to provide a random sample of 1,000 Florida residents. Of the initial sample members, 198 had moved, had incorrect addresses, were deceased, or were otherwise unreachable. These individuals were replaced with additional randomly selected residents. Thirty-three of the replacements also could not be contacted but were not replaced. Thus, the total number...was reduced to 967.”[8]

9. Researchers state that “a standardized questionnaire developed for use in this study was mailed to a stratified random sample of 750 hospitals drawn from the American Hospital Association membership list. Hospitals were stratified according to size, geographic location, and stage of managed care development....”[9]

10. A researcher states, “Surveys were mailed to a sample taken from a randomly generated list of 960 members of the School Social Work Association of America.... Sixty-seven surveys were returned....”[10]

11. Researchers state, “Children were provided with consent forms in their classrooms to take to their parents for signatures. Teachers were asked to prompt the children at the end of the school day to remember their consent form and were asked to work for 100% consent rate. Stickers were provided on the return of the consent form (endorsed yes or no). Consent forms were obtained for 100 children (45.4%).”[11]

12. Researchers state, “To randomly select parents, teachers chose every third African American child on their class list and asked selected children to take the survey to their parents.... All participants were asked to mail their completed forms in self-addressed stamped envelopes to the researchers. We offered each participant $20 for their contribution to the study. Although most participants (80%) accepted payment, some participants (11%) returned the payment to the re-

searchers.... Another 9% donated their payment to the school.... All completed surveys were individually returned by mail."[12]

13. Researchers state, "Participants were 3,446 Internet users...who had been involved in a close relationship. Each participant volunteered to complete an online questionnaire about their dating history at a Web site that features several psychological surveys...."[13]

---

[1]Greenwald. H. P., O'Keefe, S., & DiCamillo, M. (2005). Why employed Latinos lack health insurance: A study in California. *Hispanic Journal of Behavioral Sciences, 27*, 517–532.

[2]Rose, E. M., Westefeld, J. S., & Ansley, T. N. (2001). Spiritual issues in counseling: Clients' beliefs and preferences. *Journal of Counseling Psychology, 48,* 61–71.

[3]Eibach, R. P., & Ehrlinger, J. (2006). "Keep your eyes on the prize": Reference points and racial differences in assessing progress toward equality. *Personality and Social Psychology Bulletin, 32*, 66–77.

[4]Nevitt, J. R., & Lundak, J. (2005). Accuracy of self-reports of alcohol offenders in a rural midwestern county. *Psychological Reports, 96*, 511–514.

[5]Yowell, C. M. (2000). Possible selves and future orientation: Exploring hopes and fears of Latino boys and girls. *Journal of Early Adolescence, 20*, 245–280.

[6]Graue, M. E., & DiPerna, J. (2000). Redshirting and early retention: Who gets the "gift of time" and what are its outcomes? *American Educational Research Journal, 37*, 509–534.

[7]van Ryn, M., Burgess, D., Malat, J., & Griffin, J. (2006). Physicians' perceptions of patients' social and behavioral characteristics and race disparities in treatment recommendations for men with coronary artery disease. *American Journal of Public Health, 96*, 351–357.

[8]Applegate, B. K., & Davis, R. K. (2006). Public views on sentencing juvenile murderers: The impact of offender, offense, and perceived maturity. *Youth Violence and Juvenile Justice, 4*, 55–74.

[9]Mizrahi, T., & Berger, C. S. (2005). A longitudinal look at social work leadership in hospitals: The impact of a changing health care system. *Health & Social Work, 30*, 155–165.

[10]Garrett, K. J. (2005). School social workers' evaluation of group work practices. *Children & Schools, 27*, 247–256.

[11]Franz, D. Z., & Gross, A. M. (2001). Child sociometric status and parent behaviors: An observational study. *Behavior Modification, 25*, 3–20.

[12]Lambert, M. C., Puig, M., Lyubansky, M., Rowan, G. T., & Winfrey, T. (2001). Adult perspectives on behavior and emotional problems in African American children. *Journal of Black Psychology, 27*, 64–85.

[13]Swann, W. B. Jr., Sellers, J. G., McClarty, K. L. (2006). Tempting today, troubling tomorrow: The roots of the precarious couple effect. *Personality and Social Psychology Bulletin, 32*, 93–103.

Exercise 35   Treatment of Depression and Anxiety
Standard Error of the Mean and 95% Confidence Interval

Statistical Guide

The standard error of the mean (SE_M) is a margin of error to allow for when estimating the population mean from a sample drawn at random from a population. It is an allowance for chance errors created by the random sampling. When a 95% confidence interval (CI) for a mean is reported, we can have 95% confidence that the *true mean* (i.e., the mean we would get if we could eliminate sampling errors) lies within that interval. For example, if we tested a group of children with a mathematics test and got a mean of 55.00 and a 95% CI of 52.00–57.00, we could have 95% confidence that the true mean lies between these two values.

When we report a single value such as a mean based on a sample, the value is sometimes called a *point estimate* (i.e., a single point estimated to be the mean for the population based on a sample). When we report a confidence interval, we are said to be reporting an *interval estimate* (i.e., a range of values that estimate the mean for a population).

Excerpt from the Research Article[1]

Twenty-nine adult psychiatric outpatients constituted the sample. They completed a 12-session group cognitive therapy program [in small groups]. Group sizes ranged from 3 to 6 members.

The instruments used in this program included the Beck Depression Inventory (BDI)..., [which] is a widely used instrument in the evaluation of depression.... Anxiety was measured with the Beck Anxiety Inventory (BAI), a 21-item self-report instrument that measures anxiety severity for the past week, including the day of completion. The Dysfunctional Attitudes Scale (DAS)...measures identification with attitudes associated with depressive disorders....

From the pre- to posttest, the average change on the BDI was a decrease of 8.42 points.... BAI scores fell an average of 4.65 points.... For the DAS, the average change from pre- to posttest was 21.43 points. [The 95% confidence intervals for these mean change scores are given in Table 1 below.]

Table 1
Means and Standard Deviations for Outcome Measures

Measure	Pretest		Posttest		95% CI
	M	*SD*	*M*	*SD*	
BDI	21.69	10.12	13.27	9.27	4.59–12.25
BAI	17.23	11.55	12.58	9.56	0.17–9.14
DAS	156.81	33.72	135.38	35.93	6.46–36.39

Note. $N = 29$. CI = Confidence interval; BDI = Beck Depression Inventory; BAI = Beck Anxiety Inventory; DAS = Dysfunctional Attitudes Scale.

---

[1] Source: Kush, F. R., & Fleming, L. M. (2000). An innovative approach to short-term group cognitive therapy in the combined treatment of anxiety and depression. *Group Dynamics: Theory, Research, and Practice, 4*, 176–183. Copyright © 2000 by the Educational Publishing Foundation. Reprinted with permission.

Questions for Exercise 35

Part A: Factual Questions

1. The anxiety scores fell an average of how many points?

2. For your answer to Question 1 (the *point estimate*), what is the 95% confidence interval (the *interval estimate*)?

3. If you were reporting a point estimate for the mean change on the "DAS," what value or values should you report?

4. If you were reporting an interval estimate for the mean change on the "BDI," what value or values should you report?

5. For which measure does the interval estimate come closest to indicating zero change? Explain the basis for your answer.

6. Which confidence interval is largest?

7. Which confidence interval is smallest?

8. In light of the 95% confidence intervals, does the treatment appear to be effective? Explain.

Part B: Questions for Discussion

9. In your opinion, do the "point estimates given in the text" *or* the "interval estimates given in the table" provide better information about the effectiveness of the treatments? Explain.

10. In your opinion, is the sample size adequate for a study of this type? Explain.

11. Suppose a fourth variable had been measured, and the 95% confidence interval for it was −2.11 to 8.76. What would the negative value tell you about the effectiveness of the treatment?

Exercise 36 Social Traits of Hearing-Impaired Students

Standard Error of the Mean and 68%, 95%, and 99% Confidence Intervals

Statistical Guide

To review the standard error of the mean, see the statistical guide for Exercise 35. Most authors of research reports in journal articles do not report the standard error of the mean. However, they usually give you enough information so that you can compute it using the formula shown in Question 1 for this exercise.

For a 68% confidence interval, simply add the standard error of the mean to the mean and then subtract it from the mean. For a 95% confidence interval, first multiply the standard error of the mean by 1.96 and then add and subtract. For a 99% confidence interval, multiply by 2.58 before adding and subtracting. The intervals obtained using these multipliers are precise only with large samples; they become rather precise with 60 or more cases.

Excerpt from the Research Article[1]

Participants were 220 hearing-impaired adolescents enrolled in 15 large public school programs…throughout the United States and in one Canadian metropolitan area. Participants were in the high school part of the program.

Participation. Participation was tapped with four subscales: (a) One six-item subscale included items referring to participation in the classroom and in school with hearing-impaired peers (e.g., class related: "In my mainstream classes, I talk with hearing-impaired students"; school related: "I have lunch with hearing-impaired friends"). Students responded on a 5-point scale.

A second six-item subscale was identical to the first, except that the word *hearing* was substituted for *hearing-impaired* (e.g., "In my mainstream classes, I talk with hearing students").

An additional seven-item subscale dealt with participation in out-of-school social activities with hearing-impaired friends (e.g., "Go to parties at hearing-impaired friends' homes")…. A second seven-item subscale was identical to the preceding one, except *hearing* was substituted for *hearing-impaired* (e.g., "Go to parties at hearing friends' homes").

Emotional Security. Emotional security was tapped with two subscales: (a) A seven-item subscale included items referring to hearing-impaired students (e.g., "When I'm with hearing-impaired students my age, I feel nervous")…. (b) A second seven-item subscale was identical to the preceding one, except for the substitution of *hearing* for *hearing-impaired* (e.g., "When I'm with hearing students my age, I feel nervous")….

---

[1] Source: Stinson, M. S., Whitmire, K., & Kluwin, T. N. (1996). Self-perceptions of social relationships in hearing-impaired adolescents. *Journal of Educational Psychology, 88,* 132–143. Copyright © 1996 by the American Psychological Association, Inc. Reprinted with permission.

Table 1
Means and Standard Deviations

Subscale	M	SD
School Participation		
With hearing-impaired students	19.5	5.1
With hearing students	17.4	5.1
Social Activities		
With hearing-impaired students	18.5	5.6
With hearing students	19.0	5.5
Emotional Security		
With hearing-impaired students	22.2	3.7
With hearing students	21.6	3.8

Note. N for all subscales was 220. (Higher averages indicate more of the trait in question.)

Questions for Exercise 36

Part A: Factual Questions

1. What is the standard error of the mean for "School Participation with hearing-impaired students"? Calculate it using the following formula. Round your answer to two decimal places.

$$SE_M = \frac{SD}{\sqrt{N}}$$

2. What are the limits of the 68% confidence interval for "School Participation with hearing-impaired students"? Calculate your answer to two decimal places and round it to one decimal place.

3. What are the limits of the 95% confidence interval for "School Participation with hearing-impaired students"? Calculate your answer to two decimal places and round it to one decimal place.

4. What are the limits of the 95% confidence interval for "School Participation with hearing students"? Calculate your answer to two decimal places and round it to one decimal place.

5. Compare your answers to Questions 3 and 4. Do the two 95% confidence intervals overlap (i.e., are any of the values in one of the intervals included in the other)? (Note that when two intervals do *not* overlap, we can be confident that there is a reliable difference between the means.)

6. We can have 68% confidence that the true mean for "Social Activities with hearing-impaired students" lies between which two values? Calculate your answer to two decimal places and round it to one decimal place.

7. We can have 95% confidence that the true mean for "Social Activities with hearing-impaired students" lies between which two values? Calculate your answer to two decimal places and round it to one decimal place.

8. Compare your answers to Questions 6 and 7. If your work is right, the interval for Question 7 is larger than the interval for Question 6. Does this make sense? Explain.

9. Calculate the limits of the 99% confidence interval of the mean for "Social Activities with hearing-impaired students." (Note that you calculated the 68% and 95% confidence intervals for this variable in Questions 6 and 7.)

Part B: Questions for Discussion

10. Keep in mind that each of the means and standard deviations in Table 1 is based on an *N* of 220. Without performing any calculations, can you determine which variable in Table 1 has the smallest standard error of the mean associated with it? Explain.

11. Compare the two means for each of the three main variables in Table 1. Are all the differences in the direction you would have predicted before reading the excerpt? Explain.

12. Briefly explain what caused the errors being accounted for by the confidence intervals for the means.

Exercise 37   Communication in Relationships

t Test for Independent Groups: I

Statistical Guide

The *t* test is often used to test the significance of the difference between two means. It yields a value of *p*, which indicates the probability that chance or random sampling errors created the difference between the means. Most researchers declare a difference to be significant when *p* is equal to or less than .05. The lower the probability, the more significant the difference. Thus, a *p* of .01 is more significant than a *p* of .05. When a researcher declares a difference to be statistically significant, he or she is rejecting the null hypothesis. The lower the probability, the more confidence a researcher can have in rejecting the null hypothesis.

Note that the absence of footnotes with probabilities in a table that contains a number of significance tests indicates that the comparison in question is *not* statistically significant.

Excerpt from the Research Article[1]

The married sample comprised members of 100 heterosexual couples (54% were women and 46% were men) from a Midwestern university. The dating sample also consisted of members of 100 heterosexual couples (59% were women and 41% were men) from the same Midwestern university. All the married and dating couples were Euro-American. A researcher selected subjects in a haphazard fashion and asked them to complete a short survey.... The mean age of the sample was 26.7 years (*SD* = 2.6).

The Affectionate Communication Index is a 19-item index that...assesses the amount of verbal and nonverbal affectionate communication and support on a 7-point...scale, with anchors of 1 = partners *always* engage in this type of affectionate activity to 7 = partners *never* engage in this type of activity. [Thus, *lower* scores indicate *more* affectionate communication. Table 1 shows the results for the nonverbal activities.]

Table 1

Dating and Married Individuals' Reports of Nonverbal Affectionate Communication

Item		*n*	*M*	*SD*	*t*
Hold hands	Dating	100	3.7	1.9	3.3[†]
	Married	100	2.9	1.7	
Kiss on the lips	Dating	100	2.9	1.5	4.9[†]
	Married	100	2.0	1.1	
Kiss on the cheeks	Dating	100	3.6	1.6	4.5[†]
	Married	100	2.7	1.3	
Give massages to each other	Dating	100	4.2	1.8	5.0[†]
	Married	99	2.5	1.8	
Put arm around shoulder	Dating	100	3.6	1.8	4.6[†]
	Married	92	2.5	1.5	

Table 1 continued on next page →

---

[1] Source: Punyanunt-Carter, N. M. (2004). Reported affectionate communication and satisfaction in marital and dating relationships. *Psychological Reports*, *95*, 1154–1160. Copyright © 2004 by Psychological Reports. Reprinted with permission.

Table 1 *continued*

Hug each other	Dating	100	2.5	1.6	2.0*
	Married	100	2.1	1.2	
Sit close to each other	Dating	96	2.9	1.6	3.9†
	Married	100	2.0	1.6	
Look into each other's eyes	Dating	100	3.3	1.6	1.0
	Married	100	3.0	1.8	
Wink at each other	Dating	100	4.7	2.3	1.7
	Married	96	4.2	1.9	

*$p < .05$. †$p < .001$.

Questions for Exercise 37

Part A: Factual Questions

1. Which group had a higher mean score for kissing on the lips (i.e., on the average, which group reported *less* kissing on the lips)?

2. Is the difference between the two means for kissing on the lips statistically significant? If yes, at what probability level?

3. Should the null hypothesis be rejected for kissing on the lips? If yes, at what probability level?

4. Is the difference between the two means for hugging each other statistically significant? If yes, at what probability level?

5. Should the null hypothesis be rejected for hugging each other? If yes, at what probability level?

6. The differences are *not* statistically significant for which items?

7. Should the null hypothesis be rejected for winking at each other?

8. How many of the differences in Table 1 are statistically significant at the .05 level but not significant at the .001 level?

9. The differences between the means for the following items are statistically significant. For which one is the significance at a higher level? Explain your answer.

   A. The difference for hugging each other
   B. The difference for sitting close to each other

10. For which group can we reject the null hypothesis with greater confidence?

    A. The difference for hugging each other
    B. The difference for holding hands

Part B: Questions for Discussion

11. For all items for which there are statistically significant differences, the means for dating couples are higher than the means for married couples. If you had planned this study, would you have hypothesized this result? Explain.

12. The first difference for kissing on the cheeks is statistically significant at the .001 level. Logically, is it also significant at the .05 level? (Note: If you have a statistics textbook, examine the table of critical values of *t* to help you determine the answer to this question.)

13. The table contains five types of statistics (*n*, *M*, *SD*, *t*, and *p*). Which three are *descriptive statistics*? (Note: If you have a statistics textbook, you may want to consult it.)

14. The table contains five types of statistics (*n*, *M*, *SD*, *t*, and *p*). Which two are *inferential statistics*? (Note: If you have a statistics textbook, you may want to consult it.)

15. The researcher states that she selected the individuals for this study "in a haphazard fashion." What is your understanding of this term?

16. Do any of the results of this study surprise you? Are any of the results particularly interesting? Explain.

Exercise 38   Ethnic Identity of Korean Americans

t Test for Independent Groups: II

Statistical Guide

To review the *t* test, see the statistical guide for Exercise 37. Note that the *lower* the probability, the *higher* the level of statistical significance. For instance, $p < .001$ (1 in 1,000) is a higher level than $p < .01$ (1 in 100), and $p < .01$ is a higher level than $p < .05$ (5 in 100). Also, note that when probability levels are given as footnotes in a table (such as the table below), the absence of a footnote indicates that $p > .05$ (i.e., is greater than .05), and the associated difference between means is not statistically significant.

Excerpt from the Research Article[1]

The sample consisted of 217 Korean American students selected from ethnically diverse high schools in the Los Angeles area....

Phinney's 14-item Level of Ethnic Identity subscale was designed to assess the degree of ethnic identity among adolescents.... Items such as "I am happy that I am a member of the group I belong to"...and "I have a clear sense of my own ethnic background and what it means to me" [were included in the scale].

Phinney's 6-item Attitudes Toward Other Groups subscale was designed to assess attitudes toward other groups.... Respondents were asked to rate statements such as "I like meeting and getting to know people from ethnic groups other than my own."

A five-item checklist was developed to assess perceived discrimination. Items asked respondents' perception of the society's unfair treatment of their ethnic group and also the personal experience of unfair treatment.... Typical items stated "During your high school years, how often have you thought that your ethnic group is negatively stereotyped by mainstream people?"

Table 1

Means and Standard Deviations for Level of Ethnic Identity, Other-Group Attitudes, and Perceived Discrimination by Age and Gender

	Gender			Age			Total
	Male M (SD)	Female M (SD)	*t*	13–15 M (SD)	16–18 M (SD)	*t*	M (SD)
Level of ethnic identity	3.01 (.51)	2.99 (.56)	.18	2.91 (.49)	3.08 (.57)	−2.25*	3.00 (.54)
Other-group attitudes	2.83 (.60)	3.12 (.56)	−3.79***	2.98 (.55)	3.02 (.62)	−.41	2.99 (.59)
Perceived discrimination	1.90 (.75)	1.68 (.75)	2.09*	1.65 (.69)	1.89 (.80)	−2.36*	1.78 (.76)

Note. Scores for ethnic identity, attitudes, and discrimination range from 1 to 4.
*$p < .05$. ***$p < .001$.

[1] Source: Shrake, E. K., & Rhee, S. (2004). Ethnic identity as a predictor of problem behaviors among Korean American adolescents. *Adolescence, 39*, 601–622. Copyright © 2004 by Libra Publishers, Inc. Reprinted with permission.

Questions for Exercise 38

Part A: Factual Questions

1. What is the mean "Level of ethnic identity" for the total sample?

2. Do the males *or* females have a higher mean on "Perceived discrimination"?

3. Is the difference between the two means referred to in Question 2 statistically significant?

4. Should the null hypothesis for the difference between the two means referred to in Question 2 be rejected?

5. On "Other-group attitudes," is the difference between the 13–15-year-olds and the 16–18-year-olds statistically significant?

6. On "Perceived discrimination," is the difference between the 13–15-year-olds and the 16–18-year-olds statistically significant?

7. Should the null hypothesis for the difference between the two means referred to in Question 6 be rejected?

8. Four of the six values of *t* in the table have asterisks that refer the reader to a footnote. Explain why two of the values do not have an asterisk.

9. The value of *p* for the *t* test for the means of males and females for "Other-group attitudes" is "$p < .001$." What does this mean?

   A. Less than 1 in 10   B. Less than 1 in 100   C. Less than 1 in 1,000

10. Which of the following differences between males and females is significant at a lower level? Explain the basis for your answer.

    A. "Other-group attitudes"
    B. "Perceived discrimination"

Part B: Question for Discussion

11. This research was conducted with Korean adolescents in the Los Angeles area. Would you be willing to generalize the results of this study to Korean adolescents who live in other regions of the country? Why? Why not?

Exercise 39   Perceptions of Risky Driving Behaviors

t Test for Independent Groups: III

Statistical Guide

To review the *t* test, see the statistical guide for Exercise 37.

Excerpt from the Research Article[1]

The first group consisted of 1,430 student drivers enrolled in driver training programs.... The second group consisted of 880 teen drivers who had received a moving violation and were attending traffic school.

For both groups, attitudes concerning driving behaviors were covered in a series of questions. Participants were asked to rate six negative driving issues as to how dangerous they perceived them to be.... Rating scores were on a 5-point Likert-type scale, which ranged from least dangerous (1) to most dangerous (5).

Table 1
Perceptions of Risky Driving Behaviors

	M	SD	t	p
Risk of speeding				
Student drivers	3.85	1.08	−6.99	.000
Traffic violators	3.47	1.25		
Risk of drunk driving				
Student drivers	4.79	.61	−4.27	.000
Traffic violators	4.66	.77		
Risk of sleepy driving				
Student drivers	4.19	.86	−2.60	.01
Traffic violators	4.08	.95		
Risk of distracted driving				
Student drivers	3.71	.93	−1.39	.17
Traffic violators	3.65	.94		
Risk of slow driving				
Student drivers	2.65	1.18	1.43	.15
Traffic violators	2.73	1.30		
Risk of angry driving				
Student drivers	3.69	1.09	−2.58	.01
Traffic violators	3.56	1.10		

[1] Source: Sarkar, S., & Andreas, M. (2004). Acceptance of and engagement in risky driving behaviors by teenagers. *Adolescence, 39*, 687–700. Copyright © 2004 by Libra Publishers, Inc. Reprinted with permission.

Questions for Exercise 39

Part A: Factual Questions

1. On the average, the "Student drivers" perceived which behavior as being least risky?

2. On the average, did "Student drivers" *or* "Traffic violators" perceive drunk driving as being more risky? Explain.

3. Regarding drunk driving, is the difference between the "Student drivers" and the "Traffic violators" statistically significant? Explain.

4. Should the null hypothesis be rejected for the difference referred to in Question 3?

5. Regarding "Risk of distracted driving," is the difference between the "Student drivers" and the "Traffic violators" statistically significant? Explain.

6. Should the null hypothesis be rejected for the difference referred to in Question 5?

7. How many of the differences in Table 1 led to rejection of the null hypotheses?

8. How many of the differences in Table 1 are *not* statistically significant?

9. The "Traffic violators" have a higher mean than the "Student drivers" for which one of the six behaviors?

Part B: Questions for Discussion

10. The "Student drivers" have higher means on five of the six risky behaviors. Does this result surprise you? Explain.

11. Consider the two means for "Risk of sleepy driving" (4.19 and 4.08). Given that the behavior was rated on a scale from 1 to 5, do you consider this to be a "big" difference? Do you consider it to be an "important" difference?

12. Five of the values of *t* in Table 1 are negative, and one value is positive. If you have a statistics textbook, examine the material on the *t* test to see if you can determine why values of *t* are sometimes negative and sometimes positive.

13. The subtitle of this exercise is "*t* Test for Independent Groups: III." If you have a statistics textbook, look up this term and describe when it is appropriate to use an "*independent t test.*" (Note: In some books, it is called a *t* test for uncorrelated data.)

Exercise 40   Professionals' Role Perceptions

t Test for Dependent Groups: I

Statistical Guide

The *t* test for dependent groups has the same purpose as the one for independent groups (see the statistical guide for Exercise 37). When each member of one group is paired or matched with a member of the other group, the data are called "dependent," and the *t* test for *dependent groups* should be used. This test is also known as the *t* test for *correlated data* or the *t* test for *paired data*.

Note that when a set of significance tests is presented in a table, those tests without a footnote indicating significance should be regarded as being *not* significant.

Background Notes

In the following excerpt, the data are "paired" in the sense that each participant responded to each item twice: The first time, each indicated what they actually did; the second time, each indicated what they would like to do in the ideal. Thus, each pair of scores consists of the two responses of one respondent.

In Table 1, the symbol "*M%*" refers to the mean percentage of time spent (or might ideally be spent). Thus, these statistics are *means*, which can be tested with *t* tests.

Excerpt from the Research Article[1]

The study sample consisted of 183 school social workers, 137 school psychologists, and 166 school counselors. All were members of their respective national professional organizations…. Each organization provided me with mailing labels for a random sample of 400 current members. The 1,200 randomly selected professionals [were mailed] survey questionnaires…. The 486 returned surveys represent a response rate of 40.5%.

Each respondent was asked to indicate the proportion of his or her professional time actually dedicated to each of the 21 roles, as well as the proportion of professional time he or she would ideally devote to each role.

Table 1

Mean Proportion of Time School Counselors Actually and Would Ideally Devote to Each of 21 Professional Roles

	n	Actual		Ideal		
		M%	*SD*	*M%*	*SD*	*t*
1. Individual counseling	153	19.67	15.78	26.20	18.14	−5.80***
2. Group counseling	152	7.98	9.82	13.76	10.11	−8.98***
3. Crisis intervention	152	4.76	4.80	3.17	3.07	5.34***
4. Conflict resolution	152	3.76	4.46	5.74	8.66	3.54***
5. Academic advisement	152	5.74	8.66	5.11	7.98	1.82
6. Vocational interest testing	152	1.10	2.60	1.66	3.01	−2.14*
7. Academic scheduling	151	7.23	10.00	2.44	4.36	7.30***
8. College advisement	151	4.65	8.37	5.42	9.31	−1.96
9. Providing staff training	151	1.22	1.80	2.16	2.69	−5.58***
10. Program development	152	3.64	4.17	3.97	3.42	−1.26

Table 1 continued on next page →

---

[1] Source: Agresta, J. (2004). Professional role perceptions of school social workers, psychologists, and counselors. *Children & Schools*, *26*, 151–163. Copyright © 2004 by the National Association of Social Workers, Inc. Reprinted with permission.

Table 1 *continued*

11. Making referrals	152	4.59	5.18	3.58	3.81	3.45***
12. Staff meetings	152	3.34	3.83	2.13	2.80	5.50***
13. Research	152	0.77	1.58	1.38	2.69	−3.71***
14. Personal professional development	153	2.88	3.29	3.84	3.04	−3.27***
15. Parent education	153	1.36	1.73	2.88	2.87	−7.06***
16. Parent consultation	153	5.24	5.05	5.00	4.37	0.77
17. Administrator and/or teacher consultation	153	8.03	7.22	6.73	5.41	2.92**
18. Report writing	153	2.30	3.35	1.12	2.47	4.51***
19. Psychometric testing	153	0.41	1.33	0.26	0.92	1.82
20. Community outreach	152	0.90	1.60	1.78	2.97	−4.02***
21. Assessing psychosocial adjustment	152	0.99	1.76	1.21	2.06	1.57

*$p < .05$. **$p < .01$. ***$p < .001$.

Questions for Exercise 40

Part A: Factual Questions

1. What is the value of the difference between actual and ideal means for report writing?

2. Should the null hypothesis for the difference in your answer for Question 1 be rejected? Explain.

3. Is the difference in your answer for Question 1 statistically significant? Explain.

4. What is the value of the difference between actual and ideal means for "Parent consultation"?

5. Should the null hypothesis for the difference in your answer for Question 4 be rejected? Explain.

6. Is the difference in your answer for Question 4 statistically significant? Explain.

7. How many of the 21 null hypotheses underlying the tests in the table should *not* be rejected?

8. The differences for both Roles 17 and 18 are statistically significant. For which one of these roles is significance at a higher level? Explain.

9. The differences for both Roles 6 and 7 are statistically significant. For which one of these roles is significance at a higher level? Explain.

Part B: Questions for Discussion

10. The value of *t* in the excerpt for Role 16 is less than 1.00. If you have a statistics textbook, consult the table of critical values of *t* to determine whether a value of less than 1.00 is ever significant. Write your findings here.

11. Speculate on why some of the values of *t* are positive and some are negative. If you have a statistics textbook, examine the formula for *t*, which may help you determine the answer to this question.

12. The researcher reports a response rate of 40.5% for the mailed survey. Does this response rate surprise you? Explain.

13. Is the fact that the response rate of 40.5% is considerably less than 100% a matter of concern? Explain.

Exercise 41   Characteristics of New Parents

t Test for Dependent Groups: II

Statistical Guide

See the statistical guide for Exercise 40 to review *t* test for dependent groups, which is also known as the *t* test for correlated data or the *t* test for paired data. Also, see the statistical guide for Exercise 37 to review the interpretation of *t* tests.

In the excerpt below, the pairs are husbands and their wives (i.e., for each of the individuals in one group, his or her spouse is in the other group).

Excerpt from the Research Article[1]

Couples were first contacted during an early meeting of a childbirth course. Approximately 6 weeks before their due date (at Time 1), both members of each couple completed several self-report scales after a class, privately and without consulting one another. Approximately 6 months after childbirth (at Time 2), both partners completed a second set of self-report measures…. Participants' desire to become a parent was assessed only during the prenatal testing session. Parenting meaning/satisfaction and stress were assessed only postnatally.

The Desire to Become a Parent Scale…contains 12 items. Sample items include "I have a strong desire to have children."

Marital satisfaction was assessed by the Satisfaction subscale of the…Dyadic Adjustment Scale (DAS). Example items from this 10-item subscale are as follows: "Do you regret that you ever married?"…

Depressive symptoms were measured by the Center for Epidemiologic Studies–Depression Scale…. Participants indicated the frequency of depressive symptoms *within the last week*. Sample items include "I was bothered by things that usually didn't bother me."…

Parenting stress was measured by the…Parenting Stress Index. Example items are as follows: "My baby is so demanding that it exhausts me."…

Table 1
Descriptive Statistics: Means, Standard Deviations, and Matched-Pair t Tests

	Men		Women		
	M	*SD*	*M*	*SD*	*t*
Desire to become a parent (T1)	62.77	1.01	67.17	1.01	3.57**
Parent meaning/satisfaction (T2)	46.12	8.28	50.25	7.11	4.17***
Marital satisfaction (T1)	41.83	4.15	41.93	4.70	0.29
Marital satisfaction (T2)	40.17	5.60	39.52	6.70	1.33
Depression (T1)	29.27	7.78	31.37	7.66	2.32*
Depression (T2)	29.11	8.31	30.42	8.47	1.38
Parenting stress (T2)	31.00	17.70	36.00	16.94	3.41**

Note. T1 = Time 1; T2 = Time 2.
*$p < .05$. **$p < .01$. ***$p < .001$.

---

[1] Source: Rholes, W. S., Simpson, J. A., & Friedman, M. (2006). Avoidant attachment and the experience of parenting. *Personality and Social Psychology Bulletin, 32*, 275–285. Copyright © 2006 by the Society for Personality and Social Psychology, Inc. Reprinted with permission.

Questions for Exercise 41

Part A: Factual Questions

1. As is customary in journal articles, the researchers did not state null hypotheses. Write a statement of the null hypothesis for the first significance test in Table 1.

2. Should the null hypothesis that you wrote for Question 1 be rejected? Explain.

3. What is the mean difference for "Marital satisfaction" at Time 2 (i.e., the size of the difference between the means for men and women at Time 2)?

4. Should the null hypothesis for the mean difference for "Marital satisfaction" at Time 2 be rejected? Explain.

5. Is the mean difference for "Marital satisfaction" at Time 2 statistically significant? Explain.

6. On the average, did men *or* women report more parenting stress?

7. Is the mean difference between men and women on parenting stress statistically significant? Explain.

8. There are seven *t* tests reported in the table. Underlying each one is a null hypothesis. How many of the null hypotheses should be rejected?

9. For "Parenting stress," $p < .01$. What does this mean?
   A. Odds are less than 1 in 10 that sampling errors account for the difference.
   B. Odds are less than 1 in 100 that sampling errors account for the difference.
   C. Odds are less than 1 in 1,000 that sampling errors account for the difference.

Part B: Questions for Discussion

10. The difference for "Desire to become a parent" is significant at the .01 level. Is it also significant at the .05 level? (Hint: You should be able to answer this question based on your knowledge of the relationships among significance levels. If not, consult a statistics textbook if you have one.)

11. For "Marital satisfaction" at Time 1, the value of *t* is 0.29, which is less than 1.00. If you have a statistics textbook, consult the table of critical values of *t* to determine whether a value of less than 1.00 is ever significant. Write your findings here.

12. The researchers had members of each couple complete the self-report scales privately and without consulting one another. In your opinion, was it important to have them complete the scales without consulting with each other? Explain.

Exercise 42   Increasing Technology Skills

t Test for Dependent Groups with Effect Size: I

Statistical Guide

To review the meaning and interpretation of effect sizes, see the statistical guide for Exercise 21. To review the general purpose of the t test, see the statistical guide for Exercise 37. To review the meaning of dependent groups, see the statistical guide for Exercise 40.

Excerpt from the Research Article[1]

As part of an intervention program, a sample of 34 foster families received computers, Internet connections, and supportive services.

The Computer Confidence Scale (CCS) is a 13-item self-efficacy scale measuring self-reported confidence to perform computer tasks....

The Internet Confidence Scale (ICS) is a 16-item self-efficacy scale that measures self-reported confidence to use the Internet to perform a specific task...or use Internet-based communication.

Children rated their own skills from 1 (*no skills*) to 5 (*experienced user*).

Table 1
Foster Child Outcomes

	BSBF Group ($n = 40$)				
	Baseline		12 months		
Dependent variable	*M*	*SD*	*M*	*SD*	Significance of Difference/Effect Size
Computer Confidence Scale (CCS)	55.16	33.09	75.60	34.45	$t = -3.78$, $df = 39$, $p < .001$, ES = .61
Internet Confidence Scale (ICS)	55.26	44.21	94.27	42.72	$t = -7.39$, $df = 39$, $p < .001$, ES = .88
Self-rating of technology skills	2.48	1.02	3.23	.87	$t = -5.99$, $df = 39$, $p < .001$, ES = .93

Note. BSBF = Building Skills–Building Futures; ES = Effect Size.

Questions for Exercise 42

Part A: Factual Questions

1. What was the mean score on the CCS at the baseline (i.e., at the beginning of the program)?

2. On ICS, what is the difference between the mean at the baseline and the mean 12 months later?

---

[1] Source: Finn, J., Kerman, B., & LeCornec, J. (2005). Reducing the digital divide for children in foster care: First-year evaluation of the Building Skills–Building Futures Program. *Research on Social Work Practice, 15,* 470–480. Copyright © 2005 by Sage Publications. Reprinted with permission.

3. Would it be appropriate to reject the null hypothesis for the difference between the two means on "Self-Rating of technology skills"? Explain.

4. Would it be appropriate to reject the null hypothesis for the difference between the two means on the CCS? Explain.

5. The researchers report $p < .001$. What does this mean?

   A. Odds are less than 1 in 100.
   B. Odds are more than 1 in 100.
   C. Odds are less than 1 in 1,000.
   D. Odds are more than 1 in 1,000.

6. Each of the three comparisons are statistically significant at the .001 level. Are they also significant at the .05 level? (Hint: You should be able to answer this question based on your knowledge of the relationships among significance levels. If not, consult a table of critical values of *t* in a statistics textbook.)

7. The effect size is largest for which dependent variable?

8. The effect size exceeds one-half of a standard deviation unit for how many of the three comparisons? Explain.

9. Would it be appropriate to characterize the effect size for CCS as representing a small effect?

Part B: Questions for Discussion

10. The table in the excerpt contains the term "dependent variable." What is your understanding of the meaning of this term?

11. In your opinion, would it be informative to include a control group in a study such as this one? Explain.

Exercise 43 Summer Camp and Self-Esteem

t Test for Dependent Groups with Effect Size: II

Statistical Guide

To review the meaning and interpretation of effect sizes, including labels for various effect sizes, see the statistical guide for Exercise 21. To review the general purpose of the *t* test, see the statistical guide for Exercise 37. To review the meaning of dependent groups, see the statistical guide for Exercise 40. Note that *ns* is an abbreviation that means "not significant."

Excerpt from the Research Article[1]

The present study was designed to test the hypothesis that a session of summer camp would increase the self-esteem of economically disadvantaged school-age children from New York's inner-city neighborhoods. The sample included 68 American children, ages 6–12 years....

As a measure of self-esteem, the Piers-Harris Children's Self-concept Scale..., an 80-item self-report questionnaire, was administered as a pretest and posttest. Total scores for self-esteem range from 0 to 80, with higher scores reflecting more positive self-evaluations....

The scale taps six dimensions of self-esteem...: popularity (12 items), physical appearance and attributes (13), intellectual and school status (17), happiness and satisfaction (10), behavior (admission of problem behaviors) (16), and anxiety (14). On behavior and anxiety scales, higher scores indicate perception of fewer problems or less anxiety.

Size of treatment effect was based on Cohen's *d* for the overall score (*d* = .15) and for the popularity cluster scale (*d* = .25).

Table 1

t-Test Comparisons of Pre- and Posttest Performance on Piers-Harris Children's Self-concept and Cluster Scales

Piers-Harris	Pretest		Posttest		T_{67}	*p*
	M	*SD*	*M*	*SD*		
Total	61.8	11.0	63.4	11.0	−2.29	.03
Popularity	8.3	2.3	8.9	2.4	−2.54	.01
Physical	10.5	2.5	10.7	2.5	−.88	*ns*
Intellectual	14.1	2.7	14.4	2.6	−1.30	*ns*
Happiness	8.4	1.9	8.7	1.7	−1.51	*ns*
Behavior	13.1	2.9	13.2	3.0	−.57	*ns*
Anxiety	10.3	2.9	10.6	2.9	−1.23	*ns*

---

[1] Source: Readdick, C. A., & Schaller, G. R. (2005). Summer camp and self-esteem of school-age inner-city children. *Perceptual and Motor Skills, 101*, 121–130. Copyright © 2005 by Perceptual and Motor Skills. Reprinted with permission.

Questions for Exercise 43

Part A: Factual Questions

1. For popularity, the mean on the pretest was 8.3. What was it on the posttest?

2. What is the value of *p* for the difference between the pretest and posttest means for "Popularity"?

3. Would it be appropriate to reject the null hypothesis for the difference between the two means on "Popularity"?

4. Would it be appropriate to declare the difference between the two means on "Popularity" statistically significant?

5. According to the guidelines in the statistical guide for Exercise 21, the effect size for the difference between the means on "Popularity" should be labeled as (Note: Effect sizes are given in the last paragraph of the excerpt—not in the table.)

   A. large.
   B. moderate.
   C. small.
   D. trivial.

6. Is the difference between the means for the total scores statistically significant? Explain.

7. According to the guidelines in the statistical guide for Exercise 21, the effect size for the difference between the means for the total scores should be labeled as

   A. large.
   B. moderate.
   C. small.
   D. trivial.

8. Should the null hypothesis be rejected for the difference between the "Happiness" means? Explain.

9. Should the null hypothesis be rejected for the difference between the "Anxiety" means? Explain.

Part B: Questions for Discussion

10. Speculate on why the researchers reported effect sizes for only two of the seven differences.

11. All of the values of *t* in the table are negative. If you have a statistics textbook, consult it to determine why values of *t* are sometimes negative.

12. In the table, there is a subscript with the number "67" associated with the symbol *t*. Speculate on what the "67" indicates. Hint: If you have a statistics textbook, read about how the value of *t* is interpreted with a table of critical values.

Exercise 44   Correlates of School Attachment

Significance of a Correlation Coefficient: I

Statistical Guide

To review the interpretation of correlation coefficients in terms of what they indicate about the direction and strength of a relationship, see the statistical guide for Exercise 25.

For a correlation coefficient based on data for a sample randomly drawn from a population, the null hypothesis states that the observed value is a chance deviation from a true value of 0.00 in the population (i.e., the observed value of r is not truly different from 0.00). When the probability that the null hypothesis is true equals 5 or less in 100, most researchers reject it and declare the coefficient to be statistically significant (i.e., reliable). Note that the lower the probability, the more significant the relationship. Thus, $p < .01$ is more significant than $p < .05$. Also note that the absence of a probability level in a statistical table indicates that the relationship is not statistically significant.

Background Note

Except for grade point average, all variables were measured on a scale ranging from 1 to 10, with 1 representing the lowest level and 10 representing the highest level.

Excerpt from the Research Article[1]

The data on Latino youth in southwestern Minnesota were gathered through self-administered surveys.... Fourteen junior and senior high schools of varying size in the region were selected randomly and agreed to participate in the study to help identify factors leading to greater attachment to the school.

The following question was used:

How much would you like to change to a different school?

In the correlations displayed in Table 1, we can see that there is an inverse, though relatively weak, relationship between how attached a rural Latino youth in the region feels to his or her school and several of the at-risk behaviors found in existing research.

Table 1
Measures of Correlation for the Desire to Change Schools

	Desire to change schools
Frequency of smoking cigarettes	.137**
Frequency of drinking alcohol	.173**
Number of fights or violent encounters in the past 2 years	.191**
Number of times arrested by police in the past 2 years	.129
Length of time living in southwest Minnesota	−.019
Plans to attend college/university immediately after high school	−.031
Serious thoughts about suicide since being at current school	.270**

Table 1 continued on next page →

[1] Source: Diaz, J. D. (2005). School attachment among Latino youth in rural Minnesota. *Hispanic Journal of Behavioral Sciences, 27,* 300–318. Copyright © 2005 by Sage Publications. Reprinted with permission.

Table 1 *continued*

Belief that white students have an easier time fitting in and succeeding at school	.181*
Belief that teachers try their best to make all students, regardless of race, feel welcome and appreciated	−.260**
How comfortable the student feels in raising hand in class to ask a question	−.235**
The student's grade point average	−.145*
Frequency of skipping school without the knowledge of parents	.195**

*$p < .05$. **$p < .01$.

Questions for Exercise 44

Part A: Factual Questions

1. In the excerpt, the researcher refers to "inverse relationships." How many of the relationships are inverse?

2. The correlation between "The student's grade point average" and "Desire to change schools" indicates that those who are lower in GPA tend to have a

   A. lower desire to change schools.   B. higher desire to change schools.

3. Is the relationship between "Frequency of smoking cigarettes" and "Desire to change schools" direct *or* inverse?

4. Is the relationship between "How comfortable the student feels in raising hand in class to ask a question" and "Desire to change schools" direct *or* inverse?

5. Is the relationship between "Plans to attend college/university immediately after high school" and "Desire to change schools" statistically significant? Explain.

6. Should the null hypothesis for the relationship referred to in Question 5 be rejected?

7. Should the null hypothesis for the relationship between "Frequency of drinking alcohol" and "Desire to change schools" be rejected?

8. Both "Frequency of skipping school without the knowledge of parents" and "Belief that white students have an easier time fitting in and succeeding at school" are significantly related to "Desire to change schools." Which one is significant at a higher level? Explain.

9. Two of the variables are significantly related to "Desire to change schools" at the .05 probability level. How many of the other variables are significant at a higher probability level? Explain.

10. The value "$p < .01$" in a footnote to the table indicates that the probability that the null hypothesis is true is less than one in

    A. 10. B. 100. C. 1,000.

11. The value "$p < .05$" in a footnote to the table indicates that the probability that the null hypothesis is true is less than five in

    A. 10. B. 50. C. 100.

12. Which of the following coefficients from Table 1 represents the strongest relationship?

    A. .191. B. –.245. C. –.260. D. .195.

Part B: Questions for Discussion

13. In the excerpt, the researcher refers to the relationships as "relatively weak." Based on what you know about interpreting correlation coefficients, do you agree with this characterization? Explain.

14. Describe in words, without using numbers, the strength and direction of the relationship between "Plans to attend college/university immediately after high school" and "Desire to change schools."

15. Describe in words, without using numbers, the strength and direction of the relationship between "Belief that white students have an easier time fitting in and succeeding at school" and "Desire to change schools."

Exercise 45   Workaholism
Significance of a Correlation Coefficient: II

Statistical Guide

To review the Pearson r, see the statistical guide for Exercise 25. To review the coefficient of determination, see the statistical guide for Exercise 28. To review the meaning of the significance of r, see the statistical guide for Exercise 44. Keep in mind that the lower the probability, the higher the level of significance.

Background Information

Of the entire population of 4,000 employees in a high-technology company, a random sample of 503 were invited to participate in the study. Of these, 171 participated. The excerpt shown below shows a sample item from each instrument on which Table 1 is based.

Excerpt from the Research Article[1]

Potential participants ($N = 503$) were randomly selected from a database for the entire population of salaried employees…in a large, high technology corporation located in the U.S. [They were administered the following scales.]

Driven scale sample item: "I feel guilty when I take time off from work."

Work Involvement sample item: "Between my job and other activities I'm involved in, I don't have much free time."

Enjoyment of Work scale sample item: "My job is so interesting that it often doesn't seem like work."

Work-life Conflict sample item: "After work, I come home too tired to do some of the things I'd like to do."

Life Satisfaction sample item: "If I could live my life over, I would change almost nothing."

Purpose in Life sample item: "I am usually (1) *completely bored* to (7) *exuberant, enthusiastic.*"

Table 1
Summary Statistics and Intercorrelations for Workaholism Scales and Outcome Measures

Measure	Driven	WI	Enjoy	WLC	LS	PIL	M	SD
Driven	—	.24**	.00	.42**	−.20**	−.08	18.91	3.79
WI		—	.08	.20**	−.20**	.03	17.78	4.46
Enjoy			—	−.14	.37**	.42**	20.68	5.92
WLC				—	−.24**	−.17*	13.05	3.47
LS					—	.53**	21.49	6.43
PIL						—	107.23	13.54

Note. $N = 171$. WI = Work Involvement scale; Enjoy = Enjoyment of Work scale; WLC = Work-life Conflict; LS = Life Satisfaction scale; PIL = Purpose in Life scale.
*$p < .05$, two-tailed. **$p < .01$, two-tailed.

---

[1] Source: Bonebright, C. A., Clay, D. L., & Ankenmann, R. D. (2000). The relationship of workaholism with work-life conflict, life satisfaction, and purpose in life. *Journal of Counseling Psychology, 47*, 469–477. Copyright © 2000 by the American Psychological Association, Inc. Reprinted with permission.

Questions for Exercise 45

Part A: Factual Questions

1. What is the correlation coefficient for the relationship between "Life Satisfaction" and "Purpose in Life"?

2. What are the names of the two scales between which there is the weakest correlation?

3. Is the correlation coefficient for the relationship between "Enjoyment of Work" and "Purpose in Life" statistically significant? If yes, at what probability level is it significant?

4. The relationship between "WLC" and "LS" is such that those who have high "WLC" scores tend to have

   A. high "LS" scores.   B. low "LS" scores.

5. "Driven" has *in*significant relationships with which other variables? Identify them by their abbreviations.

6. There are 10 statistically significant correlation coefficients in the table. Are they all significant at the same level of significance? Explain.

7. Should the null hypothesis for the relationship between "WI" and "LS" be rejected? Explain.

8. What is the probability that the correlation for the relationship between "Enjoy" and "PIL" is a chance deviation (due to random sampling errors) from 0.00?

9. In statistics, a Type I error is the error of rejecting the null hypothesis when, in truth, it is correct. If we reject the null hypothesis regarding the relationship between "Driven" and "WI," what is the probability that we are making a Type I error?

10. How many of the correlations with "PIL" are statistically significant?

Part B: Questions for Discussion

11. Does it surprise you that some of the negative correlation coefficients are statistically significant? Explain.

12. The correlation between "WI" and "LS" is –.20, which in this study is statistically significant. Would you characterize this relationship as being "very strong"? Explain.

13. Are the values in the column labeled "*M*" correlation coefficients? Explain.

14. Does it surprise you that the relationship between "Life Satisfaction" and "Purpose in Life" is statistically significant? Explain.

Exercise 46   Correlates of Alcohol and Tobacco Use

Significance of a Correlation Coefficient: III

Statistical Guide

To review the Pearson r, see the statistical guide for Exercise 25. To review the significance of a correlation coefficient, see the statistical guide for Exercise 44.

Note that in a table in which some correlation coefficients are significant and others are not significant, those without a p value are not significant (i.e., p is greater than .05).

Excerpt from the Research Article[1]

From intact families, 321 adolescents participated in the present study…the age range for all being 12–16 years. There was no significant age difference between the sexes. Participants were asked to estimate how often (a) they, (b) their mothers, (c) their fathers, and (d) their best friends smoked tobacco and used alcoholic beverages. The estimations were made on a 5-point scale with anchors of 0: never, 1: almost never, 2: occasionally, 3: often, and 4: very often.

Table 1

Correlations for Adolescent Girls' and Boys' Tobacco and Alcohol Habits with Those of Their Mothers, Their Fathers, and Their Best Friends

	Girls' habits		Boys' habits	
	Tobacco	Alcohol	Tobacco	Alcohol
Mother smokes	.39†	.38†	.30*	.16
Mother uses alcohol	.43‡	.37†	.23	.20*
Father smokes	.22	.01	.20	.08
Father uses alcohol	.18	.39†	.42‡	.34†
Friends smoke	.52‡	.52‡	.71‡	.72‡
Friends use alcohol	.43‡	.83‡	.70‡	.76‡

$^*p < .05.$ $^\dagger p < .01.$ $^\ddagger p < .001.$

The present study corroborates previous research indicating both parental and peer influence on tobacco and alcohol consumption among adolescents. The study suggests that the influence of peers might be greater than that of parents. However, correlations as such do not suggest causal relationships. There are certainly other social psychological factors that may contribute to the explanation of or covary with adolescent alcohol and tobacco consumption.

---

[1] Source: Björkqvist, K., Båtman, A., & Åman-Back, S. (2004). Adolescents' use of tobacco and alcohol: Correlations with habits of parents and friends. *Psychological Reports*, 95, 418–420. Copyright © 2004 by Psychological Reports. Reprinted with permission.

Questions for Exercise 46

Part A: Factual Questions

1. For boys, which variable correlates most highly with their tobacco habits?

2. For girls, which variable correlates most highly with their tobacco habits?

3. Is the relationship between boys' alcohol habits and their fathers' tobacco habits strong? Explain.

4. Is the relationship between girls' alcohol habits and their friends' alcohol habits strong? Explain.

5. Is the relationship between girls' alcohol habits and their mothers' alcohol habits statistically significant? If yes, at what probability level?

6. Should the null hypothesis for the relationship referred to in Question 5 be rejected?

7. Is the relationship between boys' alcohol habits and their friends' alcohol habits statistically significant? If yes, at what probability level?

8. Should the null hypothesis for the relationship referred to in Question 7 be rejected?

9. What is the probability that the value of .39 (the r in the upper-left corner of the table) is a random deviation from a true correlation of 0.00?

10. The value of r for the relationship between girls' alcohol habits and fathers' smoking habits is .01. Does this mean the correlation coefficient is statistically significant at the .01 level? Explain.

11. The value "$p < .001$" in a footnote to the table indicates that the probability that the null hypothesis is true is less than one in

    A. 10.   B. 100.   C. 1,000.   D. 10,000.

12. Underlying the 24 correlation coefficients in the table, there are 24 null hypotheses. How many of the null hypotheses were rejected?

13. The correlation coefficient for which of the following relationships is statistically significant at a higher level? Explain the basis for your answer.

    A. The relationship between girls' smoking habits and mothers' smoking habits.
    B. The relationship between girls' smoking habits and friends' smoking habits.

14. The null hypothesis was rejected for both of the relationships in the following choices. The researchers can have greater confidence in being correct in rejecting the null hypothesis for which one? Explain the basis for your answer.

    A. The relationship between boys' alcohol habits and mothers' alcohol habits.
    B. The relationship between boys' alcohol habits and fathers' alcohol habits.

Part B: Questions for Discussion

15. If you had planned this study, would you have hypothesized that the correlations would be greater with friends' habits than with parents' habits? Explain.

16. Describe in words, without using numbers, the direction and strength of the relationship between boys' smoking habits and mothers' smoking habits.

17. The researchers point out that "correlations as such do not suggest causal relationships." In light of this, do you agree that the correlations between the participants' habits and their friends' habits might not be causal? Explain.

Exercise 47   Mathematics Anxiety Rating Scale

Test–Retest Reliability and Validity Coefficients

Statistical Guide

To review the Pearson r, see the statistical guide for Exercise 25. To review the meaning of the significance of r, see the statistical guide for Exercise 44. Keep in mind that the lower the probability, the higher the level of significance.

An important use of correlation coefficients is to describe the reliability of tests and other measurement scales such as attitude scales and personality measures. To review the meaning of *test–retest reliability*, see the statistical guide for Exercise 30.

Another important use of correlation coefficients is to describe the validity of tests and other measurement scales. The *validity* of a test refers to the extent to which the test is measuring the trait that it is supposed to measure. One method for estimating validity is to administer the test (e.g., a reading test) to a group of examinees and to obtain another set of scores on a variable that should be related to the test scores (e.g., teachers' ratings of students' reading ability). To the extent that the two variables are related in the expected direction (e.g., reading test scores are correlated with teachers' ratings of students' reading ability), the test is said to be valid. When correlation coefficients are used to describe validity, they are usually called *validity coefficients*.

Note that when the Pearson *r correlation coefficient* is used to describe reliability and validity, it is calculated using the same formula and is interpreted in the same way as any other Pearson r. Only the name is changed to *reliability coefficient* or *validity coefficient* to indicate the purpose for which it is being used.

Excerpt from the Research Article[1]

As a measure of mathematics anxiety, the Mathematics Anxiety Rating Scale (MARS) has been a major scale used for research and clinical studies since 1972.… Despite the usefulness of the original scale, researchers have sought a shorter version of the scale to reduce the administration time of the original 98-item inventory.…

The purpose of this study was to develop systematically a shorter version of the Mathematics Anxiety Rating Scale.… The study also aimed to provide information on validity and test–retest reliability for the brief [30-item] version.

The 98-item MARS (MARS 98-item) and a shorter 30-item version (MARS 30-item) were [each administered twice to] 124 female and male volunteers (63 women and 61 men), introductory psychology students…in a state university in two sessions one week apart. Introductory psychology is a broad survey course involving students in a broad range of majors.…

The 1-week test–retest reliability for the MARS 30-item version was .90 ($p < .001$), which is equivalent to the test–retest reliability of .91 ($p < .001$) of the longer MARS 98-item obtained during this study.

…validity for the MARS 30-item version was first measured by calculating Pearson correlations with the MARS 98-item scale. Tests from both Weeks 1 and 2 correlated significantly. At Week 1, $r = .92$ ($p < .001$) between the two scales, and at Week 2, $r = .94$ ($p < .001$).

---

[1] Source: Suinn, R. M., & Winston, E. H. (2003). The Mathematics Anxiety Rating Scale, a brief version: Psychometric data. *Psychological Reports*, *92*, 167–173. Copyright © 2003 by Psychological Reports. Reprinted with permission.

As further validation, it was predicted that high scores on mathematics anxiety would be negatively correlated with grade point average (GPA) in mathematics courses since mathematics anxiety is presumed to interfere with mathematics performance. Results were as predicted. Correlations between each of the measures of mathematics anxiety (MARS 30-item first testing, MARS 30-item second testing, MARS 98-item first testing, MARS 98-item second testing) and grades in high school mathematics courses were, respectively, $-.41$ ($p < .001$), $-.31$ ($p < .007$), $-.46$ ($p < .001$), and $-.34$ ($p < .003$). Thus, high scores on mathematics anxiety were significantly negatively correlated with mathematics performance in high school; the shorter and the longer scales actually showing similar magnitudes.

Questions for Exercise 47

Part A: Factual Questions

1. In order to estimate reliability, each version of the MARS (i.e., 30-item and 98-item) was administered twice. How many weeks separated the two administrations?

2. What is the value of the test–retest reliability coefficient for the MARS 98-item version?

3. Were the test–retest reliability coefficients for the two versions of the scale comparable? Explain.

4. What was done to first measure validity for the MARS 30-item?

5. At Week 1, the students took both the long and the short versions of MARS. Were the two sets of scores obtained at that time highly correlated? Explain.

6. At Week 2, the students took both the long and the short versions of MARS for a second time. Is the correlation coefficient for this administration of the two tests statistically significant? If yes, at what probability level?

7. A correlation coefficient of .94 is reported for Week 2 in the excerpt. Would most researchers reject the null hypothesis for it?

8. What is the reason the researchers gave for predicting that the correlation between scores on mathematics anxiety and grade point average in mathematics courses would be negative (i.e., inverse)?

9. What was the value of the validity coefficient between MARS 30-item first testing and grades in high school mathematics courses?

10. Is the validity coefficient you reported as an answer to Question 9 statistically significant? If yes, at what probability level?

Part B: Questions for Discussion

11. To what extent do you think the results reported here apply to all introductory psychology students in the United States?

12. For test–retest reliability, the researchers waited one week between the two administrations. If you have a statistics textbook that discusses test–retest reliability, what interval does the textbook author recommend?

13. Two types of validity studies are reported in the excerpt. In the first study, the MARS 30-item scores were correlated with the MARS 98-item scores. Does it surprise you that the correlations were very high (i.e., .92 on the first administration of the two scales and .94 on the second administration)?

14. In the second validity study, the MARS scores were correlated with grades in high school mathematics courses. The correlations were negative in value. Does it surprise you that they were negative? Explain.

15. In the second validity study, the validity coefficients were not only negative in value but also much more modest in value than in the first validity study. Does it surprise you that they were only modest in this validity study?

Exercise 48   A Measure of Prosocial Tendencies

Internal Consistency and Test–Retest Reliability

Statistical Guide

To review the Pearson r, see the statistical guide for Exercise 25. To review the meaning of the significance of r, see the statistical guide for Exercise 44. Keep in mind that the lower the probability, the higher the level of significance.

To review test–retest reliability, see the statistical guide for Exercise 30.

Internal consistency refers to the extent to which the items in a test measure the same trait. For tests designed to measure a single trait (e.g., knowledge of facts relating to the Civil War), one would expect internally consistent results such that examinees who do well on one test item would do well on any other test item. In addition, if there is internal consistency within a test, one would also expect that examinees who do not do well on any one test item would not do well on any other test item. Lack of internal consistency for a test designed to measure a single trait suggests that there is something wrong with the test, such as ambiguous or otherwise poorly written test items.

Note that an examinee's score on each item in a test can be designated as "0" for "wrong" and "1" for "right." Consider the first and second items on a test. If Jose has both of them right while Jennifer has both of them wrong, this would suggest internally consistent results (i.e., what we learn about Jose from the first item is the same as what we learn about him from the second item). On the other hand, if Jose and Jennifer each have one item right and the other item wrong, this would suggest that the test items are not internally consistent.

Across a large group of examinees who take a test with many items, it is difficult to determine the internal consistency of results by examining all the "rights" and "wrongs." Instead, researchers compute Cronbach's alpha (α), which is a correlation coefficient that describes the average of all the internal correlations among the items on a test.[1] In practice, coefficient alpha ranges from 0.00 (total absence of consistency from item to item) to 1.00 (perfect consistency).

Excerpt from the Research Article[2]

The six types of prosocial behaviors in the PTM-R [Prosocial Tendencies Measure–Revised] include public, anonymous, dire, emotional, compliant, and altruism.… Public prosocial behaviors were defined as behaviors intended to benefit others enacted in the presence of others (four items; sample item, "I can help others best when people are watching me"). Anonymous prosocial behaviors were defined as the tendency to help others without other people's knowledge (five items; "I think that helping others without them knowing is the best type of situation"). Dire prosocial behaviors refer to helping others under emergency or crisis situations (three items; "I tend to help people who are in real crisis or need"). Emotional prosocial behaviors are behaviors intended to benefit others enacted under emotionally evocative situations (five items; "I respond to helping others best when the situation is highly emotional"). Compliant prosocial behaviors refer to helping others when asked to (two items; "When people ask me to help them, I don't hesitate"). Altruism refers to helping others when there is little or no perceived potential for a direct, explicit reward to the self (six

---

[1] For those who are familiar with split-half reliability, note that alpha is the adjusted average correlation among all the possible splits of the items on a test.

[2] Source: Carlo, G., Hausmann, A., Christiansen, S., & Randall, B. A. (2003). Sociocognitive and behavioral correlates of a measure of prosocial tendencies for adolescents. *Journal of Early Adolescence, 23,* 107–134. Copyright © 2003 by Sage Publications. Reprinted with permission.

items; "I often help even if I don't think I will get anything out of helping"). Data were coded such that high scores on each of these scales reflect a stronger endorsement. The scoring key and instructions for the PTM-R can be obtained on request from the first author.

Table 1
Cronbach's Alphas and Test–Retest Reliabilities for the PTM-R Scales by Age Group

Variable	# of items	Cronbach's alpha		Test–retest reliabilities	
		Early adolescents	Middle adolescents	Early adolescents	Middle adolescents
Compliant	2	.80	.75	.64	.73
Public	4	.76	.86	.54	.56
Anonymous	5	.76	.84	.66	.78
Dire	3	.71	.75	.72	.63
Emotional	5	.86	.82	.72	.82
Altruism	6	.59	.80	.76	.73

Questions for Exercise 48

Part A: Factual Questions

1. Which variable had the largest number of items?

2. Which variable had the smallest number of items?

3. Traditionally, authors of textbooks on tests and measurements have suggested that, at a minimum, a test should have a reliability of .70 to be considered sufficiently reliable to use for the assessment of individuals. Using this criterion when evaluating the test–retest reliability coefficients for middle adolescents, which variables measured by the test are sufficiently reliable?

4. For early adolescents, which variable is the most reliable in terms of test–retest reliability?

5. For early adolescents, which variable is the least reliable in terms of its test–retest coefficient?

6. For early adolescents, which variable exhibited the most internal consistency?

7. For middle adolescents, which variable exhibited the most internal consistency?

8. What is the value of Cronbach's alpha for the variable "Dire" for early adolescents?

Part B: Questions for Discussion

9. A general principle in the field of tests and measurements is that longer tests *tend to be* more re-liable than shorter ones. In your opinion, is that principle illustrated by the reliability coefficients shown in the table?

10. Describe in your own words the strength of the reliability coefficient for the variable "Public" for the two groups of adolescents.

11. The researchers calculated the values of Cronbach's alpha separately for each of the six vari-ables. Speculate on why they did this instead of calculating a single value of alpha for all items on the PTM-R.

12. It would be possible for the examinees to give socially desirable responses to the items even if those responses were not true. If this occurred, do you think it would lower the measure's test–retest reliability?

Exercise 49   Extracurricular Activities and Dropping Out

One-Way ANOVA

Statistical Guide

Like a *t* test, a one-way analysis of variance (ANOVA) can be used to determine the significance of the difference between two means. Instead of yielding a value of *t*, however, an ANOVA yields a value of *F*. For a given set of data, *t* and *F* will yield the same probability (*p*) that the null hypothesis is true. Thus, the two tests are interchangeable when comparing two means. As with the *t* test, when an ANOVA yields a small value of *p* (such as .05, .01, or .001), the null hypothesis is rejected. A one-way ANOVA is also known as a univariate ANOVA.

Excerpt from the Research Article[1]

This study examined the relation between involvement in school-based extracurricular activities and early school dropout. Longitudinal assessments were completed for 392 adolescents (206 girls, 186 boys).... *Early school dropout* was defined as failure to complete the 11th grade.

To evaluate whether extracurricular involvement would predict early school dropout, we compared activity participation across grades 7 to 10 for dropouts and nondropouts. Univariate ANOVAs were performed separately at each grade.... Figure 2 shows the mean number of activities participated in by nondropouts and dropouts. Dropouts participated in significantly fewer extracurricular activities at all grades, even several years prior to dropout; 7th grade, $F(1, 389) = 8.41$, $p < .01$; 8th grade, $F(1, 365) = 10.14$, $p < .001$; 9th grade, $F(1, 343) = 15.46$, $p < .001$; and 10th grade, $F(1, 314) = 31.00$, $p < .001$.

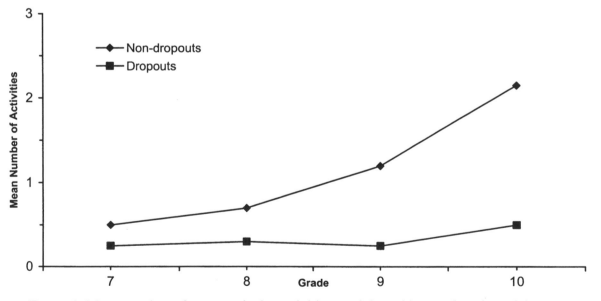

Figure 2. Mean number of extracurricular activities participated in as a function of dropout status and grade.

---

[1] Source: Mahoney, J. L., & Cairns, R. B. (1997). Do extracurricular activities protect against early school dropout? *Developmental Psychology, 33*, 241–253. Copyright © 1997 by the American Psychological Association, Inc. Reprinted with permission.

Questions for Exercise 49

Part A: Factual Questions

1. According to Figure 2, at which grade level was the average number of extracurricular activities for dropouts the most similar to the average number for nondropouts?

2. Is the difference referred to in Question 1 statistically significant? If yes, at what probability level is it significant?

3. Should the null hypothesis be rejected for the difference referred to in Question 1? If so, at what probability level should it be rejected?

4. What is the probability that random sampling errors created the mean difference between the two groups at the 8th grade level?

5. Should the null hypothesis be rejected for the difference between the two means at the 9th grade level? Explain.

6. How many means are being compared at each grade level?

7. The difference at the 7th grade is

   A. more statistically significant than the differences at the other grade levels.
   B. less statistically significant than the differences at the other grade levels.

Part B: Questions for Discussion

8. The researchers indicate that their study was *longitudinal*. What do you think this term means?

9. The researchers do not report the standard deviations associated with the means. Would you be interested in knowing the standard deviations? Explain.

10. If you have studied how to compute an ANOVA, explain the meaning of the values in parentheses immediately after each F. In other words, what is the name for these values, and on what are they based?

11. In your opinion, have the researchers established that participation in extracurricular activities *causes* a reduction in dropping out? Explain.

Exercise 50   Race/Ethnicity and Self-Esteem

One-Way ANOVA with Post Hoc Tests

Statistical Guide

To review the one-way ANOVA, see the statistical guide for Exercise 49. Note that a one-way ANOVA indicates only if a set of differences is statistically significant. For instance, if an ANOVA indicates that the set of mean differences among Groups A, B, and C is significant, it does not indicate which of the following pairs are significant: (1) A versus B, (2) A versus C, and (3) B versus C. In other words, the significant ANOVA indicates only that one or more of these pairs is significant. To pinpoint which pairs(s) are significant, post hoc tests (also known as multiple-comparisons tests) are used. There are several post hoc tests, one of which, known as Duncan's test, is reported below. Note that post hoc tests are run only to compare pairs of means in a set that has first been identified as statistically significant with an ANOVA.

Background Notes

A one-way ANOVA was run for each row in the table in the excerpt. For each, a value of F is shown. Duncan's test was also run for each row. In a given row, entries with superscript ([a]) have significantly different means from entries with superscript ([b]). Note that as a general rule if there is no indication that a difference (or a set of differences) is significant, the reader should assume that it is not significant.

Excerpt from the Research Article[1]

As part of a larger study of family functioning, a total of 104 families (adolescents, mothers, and fathers) participated in this study. All participating families in the current study included an adolescent, the mother, and the father. Adolescents were required to have at least monthly face-to-face contact with their biological mother and their biological father for inclusion....

Participants completed the age-appropriate version of the Harter Self-Perception Profiles, which conceptualize self-esteem as perceived competence in multiple domains. The social acceptance domain assesses participants' perceptions of feeling accepted by peers, feeling popular, and feeling comfortable around others. The physical appearance domain assesses participants' self-perceptions of their attractiveness and their satisfaction with their appearance. The athletic competence domain assesses participants' feelings of their competence in sports and other physical activities. The global self-worth subscale assesses participants' feelings about themselves overall (i.e., not tied to any specific domain...).

In order to test for the racial/ethnic group differences..., a series of ANOVAs was completed for each informant (adolescents, mothers, and fathers). Significant ANOVAs were followed up by post hoc Duncan's tests.

---

[1] Source: Phares, V., Fields, S., Watkins-Clay, M. M., Kamboukos, D., & Han, S. (2005). Race/ethnicity and self-esteem in families of adolescents. *Child & Family Behavior Therapy, 27*, 13–26. Copyright © 2005 by The Haworth Press, Inc. Reprinted with permission.

Table 1
Means and Standard Deviations for Self-Esteem

| | Race/ethnicity | | | |
	Caucasian	African American	Hispanic/Latino/Latina	F-Value
Social acceptance				
Adolescents	3.15 (.76)	3.13 (.74)	3.38 (.51)	1.17
Mothers	3.23 (.67)	3.44 (.55)	3.25 (.60)	1.21
Fathers	2.98 (.71)	3.36 (.62)	3.20 (.66)	2.81
Physical appearance				
Adolescents	2.82 (.85)	3.06 (.77)	2.92 (.75)	0.81
Mothers	2.49 (.84)	2.82 (.84)	2.70 (.70)	1.56
Fathers	2.79 (.51)[a]	3.14 (.82)[b]	3.13 (.65)[b]	3.16*
Athletic competence				
Adolescents	2.79 (.87)	2.96 (.80)	3.18 (.66)	1.96
Mothers	2.04 (.79)[a]	2.49 (.78)[b]	2.07 (.64)[a]	3.95*
Fathers	2.79 (.58)	2.90 (.68)	2.88 (.75)	0.27
Global self-worth				
Adolescents	3.34 (.60)	3.35 (.66)	3.25 (.65)	0.23
Mothers	3.17 (.76)	3.32 (.67)	3.24 (.71)	0.39
Fathers	2.96 (.62)[a]	3.33 (.72)[b]	3.38 (.53)[b]	4.59*

Note. Standard deviations are in parentheses. Different superscripts signify significant mean differences.
*$p < .05$.

Questions for Exercise 50

Part A: Factual Questions

1. What is the mean score on "Athletic competence" for Caucasians?

2. According to the ANOVA, should the set of three means for adolescents on "Physical appearance" be declared to be statistically significant? Explain.

3. According to the ANOVA, should the set of three means for fathers on "Physical appearance" be declared to be statistically significant? Explain.

4. According to the ANOVA, should the null hypothesis for the set of three means for mothers on "Global self-worth" be rejected? Explain.

5. According to the ANOVA, should the null hypothesis for the set of three means for fathers on "Global self-worth" be rejected? Explain.

6. Table 1 reports on 12 ANOVAs. How many of them are statistically significant? Explain the basis for your answer.

7. According to the post hoc tests, which of the following pairs of means for mothers on "Athletic competence" are significantly different? (Circle one or more.)

   A. The difference between Caucasian and African American.
   B. The difference between Caucasian and Hispanic/Latino/Latina.
   C. The difference between African American and Hispanic/Latino/Latina.

8. According to the post hoc tests, which of the following pairs of means for fathers on "Physical appearance" are significantly different? (Circle one or more.)

   A. The difference between Caucasian and African American.
   B. The difference between Caucasian and Hispanic/Latino/Latina.
   C. The difference between African American and Hispanic/Latino/Latina.

9. According to the post hoc tests, which of the following pairs of means for fathers on "Global self-worth" are significantly different? (Circle one or more.)

   A. The difference between Caucasian and African American.
   B. The difference between Caucasian and Hispanic/Latino/Latina.
   C. The difference between African American and Hispanic/Latino/Latina.

Part B: Questions for Discussion

10. Would you be interested in knowing whether the three racial/ethnic groups differed on relevant demographics? Explain.

11. In light of the total sample size ($n = 104$ families), do you consider this study to be definitive?

Exercise 51 Effectiveness of Assertiveness Training
Two-Way ANOVA: I

Statistical Guide

To review the general purpose of ANOVA, see the statistical guide for Exercise 49. In a two-way ANOVA, there are two independent variables (usually nominal classification variables) and one outcome variable (usually a continuous score variable). To understand this, examine Figure 1 in the excerpt, where time of testing (pretest and posttest) is one of the classification variables, and level of nursing (nursing assistants, licensed vocational nurses, and registered nurses) is the other one. The outcome variable is discomfort scores.

A two-way ANOVA allows us to examine interactions between the independent variables. For example, if the different types of nurses responded differently to the treatments given between the pretest and posttest, we would say that there is an interaction (i.e., the treatments interacted with level of nursing skill).

Excerpt from the Research Article[1]

The participants in this study were the 62 members of the nursing staff working in a 47-bed Department of Veterans Affairs spinal cord injury center.

The purpose of this study was to evaluate the effectiveness of the training course in [reducing discomfort when engaging in difficult] staff interactions. A behavioral approach was selected as the basis for the training. It consisted of a combination of techniques such as lecture and discussion, modeling, and behavior rehearsal, with feedback provided by group members and the trainers....

The study included the Spinal Cord Injury Assertiveness Inventory (SCIAI) as preprogram and postprogram measures to assess the effectiveness of the training.... At the request of the nurse managers, all nursing staff participated in the training, so we had no control group.

A repeated measures ANOVA on the total score of the SCIAI showed no simple effect [i.e., main effect, $p = .1069$] related to the time of testing [i.e., the mean on the pretest ($M = 2.40$) for all participants was not significantly different from the mean on the posttest for all participants ($M = 2.27$)].... However, when we examined the participants' education, we found a statistically significant interaction effect between the time of testing and education ($F_{2,58} = 3.468$, $p = .0378$) (see Figure 1). After the class, the NAs (nursing assistants), all of whom had a high school education, showed an increased discomfort level, whereas the discomfort level of the LVNs (licensed vocational nurses) and the RNs (registered nurses) decreased. However, paired t tests on the various groups' data showed that only the RNs ($t = 2.692$, $df = 36$, $p = .0107$) exhibited a statistically significant change in their discomfort level related to time of testing.

---

[1] Source: Dunn, M., & Sommer, N. (1997). Managing difficult staff interactions: Effectiveness of assertiveness training for SCI nursing staff. *Rehabilitation Nursing, 22*, 82–87. Reprinted from *Rehabilitation Nursing, 22* (2), 82–87 with permission of the Association of Rehabilitation Nurses, 4700 West Lake Avenue, Glenview, IL 60025-1485. Copyright © 1997.

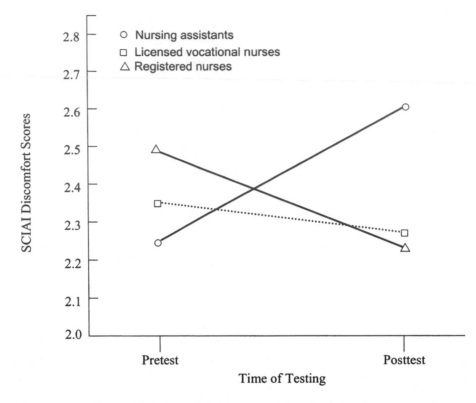

Figure 1. Interaction between time of testing (pretest vs. post-test) and educational level.

Questions for Exercise 51

Part A: Factual Questions

1. Should the null hypothesis for the main effect (for time of testing) be rejected? Explain.

2. Does Figure 1 indicate that there is an interaction? Explain.

3. Is the interaction statistically significant at the .05 level?

4. Is the interaction statistically significant at the .01 level?

5. What is the precise probability that the null hypothesis regarding the interaction is true?

6. Did the discomfort of the nursing assistants change significantly from pretest to posttest? Explain.

7. Should the null hypothesis regarding the change in the registered nurses' level of discomfort be rejected? Explain.

Part B: Questions for Discussion

8. If the findings are correct, would it be desirable to use the training with all types of nurses in the future? Explain.

9. The authors could not use a control group. Is this a limitation of the study? Explain.

10. Suppose you conducted a similar study but used a different type of training that produced a reduction in discomfort scores equally strong in all three groups of nurses. Draw a figure like the one in the excerpt showing this hypothetical result.

Exercise 52   Aggression, Gender, and Ethnicity

Two-Way ANOVA: II

Statistical Guide

To review the general purpose of ANOVA, see the statistical guide for Exercise 49. To review the more specific purpose of a two-way ANOVA, see the statistical guide for Exercise 51.

In the excerpt, the main effect for gender (as indicated by F_{gender}) is based on a comparison of the mean for all women and the mean for all men. The main effect for ethnicity (as indicated by $F_{ethnicity}$) is based on a comparison of the mean for all Anglos and the mean for all Hispanics.

Excerpt from the Research Article[1]

Subjects were 259 female and 102 male students (plus two who did not indicate their gender) who were enrolled in 11 undergraduate and 2 graduate classes at a large urban university...with a median age of 24.

The instrument was an anonymous questionnaire [that included] a list of 18 experiences and asked [the subjects] to indicate how many times they had "ever had each of the following experiences." Responses were coded as 0 (*if it has never happened to you*), 1 (*if it has happened to you once or twice*), 2 (*3 to 5 times*), 3 (*6 to 10 times*), and 4 (*more than 10 times*).

Table 1 presents the mean scores of male and female Anglos and Hispanics in their responses to the questions about the frequency with which they had experienced each of the 18 types of aggression.... None of the interactions between ethnicity and gender approached significance.

Table 1
Mean Scores for Anglo and Hispanic Males and Females on Experiences As Target

Item	Males		Females		F^a_{gender}	$F^a_{ethnicity}$
	Anglo	Hisp.	Anglo	Hisp.		
Something thrown at you	2.54	2.05	1.38	1.15	48.15***	3.79
Pushed, grabbed, shoved	2.89	2.62	2.09	1.73	24.07***	4.08*
Slapped	1.67	1.29	1.19	0.94	7.15**	3.13
Kicked, bitten, hit by fist	2.46	2.38	1.14	0.89	60.68***	1.47
Hit with object	2.18	1.95	0.93	0.85	52.52***	0.48
Beaten up	0.97	1.05	0.34	0.40	24.11***	0.27
Threatened with gun or knife	0.67	0.62	0.22	0.13	28.57***	0.91
Knife or gun used against you	0.38	0.24	0.06	0.05	19.84***	0.59
Teased meanly	2.83	2.48	2.63	1.90	2.83	12.28***
Yelled at	3.25	2.95	3.34	2.95	0.16	5.52*
Called cruel, unethical, dishonest	1.08	1.24	0.78	0.75	5.39*	0.03
Called stupid, worthless	1.75	1.00	1.59	1.38	0.01	3.32
Called an obscene name	2.92	2.76	2.32	1.84	13.85***	4.82*
Received an obscene gesture	3.10	2.57	2.45	1.92	14.69***	9.91**
Forced to have sex	0.07	0.05	0.58	0.25	16.70***	5.65*
Treated condescendingly	2.20	1.76	2.51	1.38	0.45	25.55***
Honked at loudly	2.44	2.10	2.50	1.65	0.19	17.85***
Race, culture insulted	1.58	2.05	0.96	0.93	20.37***	0.42

^{a}Degrees of freedom range from 1 and 292 to 1 and 299.

*$p < .05$. **$p < .01$. ***$p < .001$.

[1] Source: Reprinted with permission from Harris, M. B. (1996). Aggressive experiences and aggressiveness: Relationship to ethnicity, gender, and age. *Journal of Applied Social Psychology*, *26*, 843–870. © V. H. Winston & Son, Inc., 360 South Ocean Boulevard, Palm Beach, FL 33480. All rights reserved.

Questions for Exercise 52

Part A: Factual Questions

1. The average male Hispanic had something thrown at him about how many times?

2. Was there a significant difference on having "Something thrown at you" between the two ethnic groups? Explain.

3. How many means were compared by the ANOVA to get the *F* value of 24.07 for "Pushed, grabbed, shoved"?

4. How many means were compared by the ANOVA to get the *F* value of 4.08 for "Pushed, grabbed, shoved"?

5. Overall, did the "average male" *or* "average female" experience having his or her race/culture insulted more often? Explain.

6. Should the null hypothesis be rejected for the difference referred to in Question 5?

7. The average Anglo reported (a) a greater incidence of being "Teased meanly" and (b) a greater incidence of being "Yelled at" than the average Hispanic. Which of these two differences is significant at a higher level? Explain.

8. Were "more of the gender differences" *or* "more of the ethnic differences" statistically significant? Explain.

9. In all, how many null hypotheses should be rejected based on the information in Table 1?

Part B: Questions for Discussion

10. Why do you think the researcher did not give the *p* values for the interactions?

11. Examine the means for the first item in Table 1. Rewrite them in this table:

	Anglo	Hispanic
Males	$M =$	$M =$
Females	$M =$	$M =$

   Do you prefer this type of table *or* Table 1 in the excerpt for reporting the means? Explain.

12. Is it possible to determine from the excerpt (including Table 1) whether the difference between the means for Anglo males and Hispanic males on "Treated condescendingly" is statistically significant? Explain.

13. Would you be willing to generalize the results to Hispanics and Anglos enrolled in other large urban universities? Explain.

14. Are the results interesting to you? Explain.

Exercise 53   Attitudes and Beliefs About Cigars

Percentage and 95% Confidence Interval

Statistical Guide

To review percentages, see the statistical guide for Exercise 1.

A confidence interval indicates how many points should be allowed for sampling errors (i.e., errors created by random sampling from a population). The 95% confidence interval is one of the most commonly reported intervals. For instance, suppose a researcher found that 45% of respondents in a sample from a population believe that the economy is improving. Suppose further that the researcher computed the 95% confidence interval for this percentage and found that it equals 42% to 48%. Then, the research can state with 95% confidence that the true percentage in the population that believes that the economy is improving is between 42% and 48%. Note that 42% and 48% (the end points of the confidence interval) are referred to as the *limits* of the confidence interval.

Because confidence intervals are estimates of the true values in populations, when the intervals for two groups on the same question overlap, a researcher should conclude that he or she has failed to establish a *reliable difference*. Conversely, if the two intervals do *not* overlap, then a researcher should conclude that a *reliable difference* has been identified. In short, comparing confidence intervals is a type of informal significance test. Various formal significance tests are covered in a number of exercises throughout this book.

Background Notes

In Table 1 on the next page, the term "lifetime use" refers to having ever smoked cigars, while "current use" refers to smoking cigars within the past month. Also, in Table 1, "all" refers to the total sample. Furthermore, the researchers use N as the symbol for the number of students in the total sample and use n for the number of students in each subgroup. Finally, note that CI is the abbreviation for "confidence interval."

Excerpt from the Research Article[1]

Schools were recruited by letters and phone calls to health coordinators in public middle and high schools across Massachusetts and were offered survey results in exchange for participation. Twelve schools responded. We strove to administer the survey to all students in a given school, but this proved impossible in many instances because of other demands [on students' time].... Participants are the 5,016 7th through 12th graders from 12 schools....

---

[1] Source: Soldz, S., & Dorsey, E. (2005). Youth attitudes and beliefs toward alternative tobacco products: Cigars, bidis, and kreteks. *Health Education & Behavior, 32,* 549–566. Copyright © 2005 by SOPHE. Reprinted with permission.

Table 1
Endorsement Rates for Attitudes and Beliefs About Cigars

| | All | Use | | | Gender | | School Level | |
| | | No use | Lifetime use | Current use | Male | Female | Middle | High |
Cigar attitudes	(*N* = 5,016) % (95% CI)	(*n* = 4,101) % (95% CI)	(*n* = 620) % (95% CI)	(*n* = 295) % (95% CI)	(*n* = 2,451) % (95% CI)	(*n* = 2,565) % (95% CI)	(*n* = 1,985) % (95% CI)	(*n* = 3,031) % (95% CI)
Cigars taste good	11.4 (10.2–12.7)	1.6 (1.3–2.0)	44.9 (40.5–49.3)	74.0 (68.5–78.8)	18.9 (16.7–21.3)	4.3 (3.5–5.2)	5.5 (4.4–6.9)	15.2 (13.6–17.0)
Cigars smell good	23.1 (21.4–24.9)	15.3 (14.0–16.7)	52.1 (48.1–56.1)	69.1 (63.4–74.2)	30.1 (27.5–32.8)	16.4 (14.8–18.2)	14.5 (12.8–16.5)	28.7 (26.5–30.9)
Successful people smoke cigars	12.5 (11.6–13.4)	10.0 (9.1–11.0)	20.8 (17.8–24.1)	28.9 (23.8–34.5)	18.2 (16.6–20.0)	7.0 (6.0–8.1)	11.3 (10.0–12.9)	13.2 (12.1–14.4)
Cigars are not as bad for you as cigarettes	12.2 (11.2–13.2)	9.1 (8.2–10.0)	21.9 (18.6–25.7)	34.9 (30.0–40.2)	16.1 (14.6–17.7)	8.5 (7.3–9.8)	10.1 (8.8–11.5)	13.6 (12.3–14.9)
Cigars are cheaper than cigarettes	8.5 (7.6–9.5)	4.5 (3.8–5.3)	20.4 (17.1–24.0)	39.0 (33.3–45.0)	11.1 (9.7–12.6)	6.1 (5.1–7.2)	6.3 (5.0–8.0)	10.0 (8.8–11.2)
Cigars give you a good buzz	4.6 (4.0–5.3)	2.2 (1.8–2.7)	11.3 (9.2–13.8)	23.5 (18.7–29.1)	6.7 (5.7–7.8)	2.7 (2.1–3.4)	3.6 (2.8–4.6)	5.3 (4.5–6.2)
Cigars are something different to try	20.2 (18.6–21.8)	11.9 (10.7–13.2)	52.9 (48.9–56.9)	64.3 (58.5–69.6)	26.4 (24.0–28.8)	14.3 (12.7–16.0)	13.4 (11.6–15.4)	24.6 (22.6–26.7)

Note. CI = confidence interval.

Questions for Exercise 53

Part A: Factual Questions

1. How many of the 5,016 students in this study were in middle school?

2. What percentage of the middle school students endorsed the statement that "Cigars smell good"?

3. What percentage of the high school students endorsed the statement that "Cigars smell good"?

4. Did a higher percentage of the males *or* the females endorse the statement that "Cigars give you a good buzz"?

5. What are the limits of the 95% confidence interval for the "No use" group in response to the statement that "Cigars smell good"?

6. What are the limits of the 95% confidence interval for the "Current use" group in response to the statement that "Cigars smell good"?

7. The limits of the 95% confidence interval for males for the statement "Cigars taste good" are 16.7 and 21.3. Does this interval overlap with the 95% confidence interval for females in response to the same statement (i.e., are any of the values in the interval for females included in the interval for males)?

8. Based on your response to Question 7, should a researcher conclude that the difference between males and females in response to "Cigars taste good" is *reliable*? Explain the basis for your answer.

9. The limits of the 95% confidence interval for middle school students for the statement "Successful people smoke cigars" are 10.0 and 12.9. Does this interval overlap with the 95% confidence interval for high school students in response to the same statement (i.e., are any of the values in the interval for middle school students included in the interval for high school students)?

10. Based on your response to Question 9, should a researcher conclude that the difference between middle school students and high school students in response to "Successful people smoke cigars" is *reliable*? Explain the basis for your answer.

Part B: Questions for Discussion

11. Compare your answers to Questions 5 and 6. Does the difference between the two answers surprise you? Why? Why not?

12. Based on an examination of the confidence intervals, all of the differences between males and females are reliable. Does this surprise you? Why? Why not?

13. The highest endorsement rate for the total sample was in response to the statement that "Cigars are something different to try" (20.2%). Does this surprise you? Why? Why not?

Exercise 54   Types of Child Abuse

Standard Error of a Percentage and Confidence Interval

Statistical Guide

To review percentages, see the statistical guide for Exercise 1. The standard error of a percentage is a margin of error (i.e., an allowance for error that we use when estimating the population percentage from a sample drawn at random from a population). For instance, if 60% of a sample from a population answers "yes" to a survey question and the standard error of the percentage is 3 percentage points, we should allow 3 points on each side of 60% for sampling error. More specifically, we could say that there is a 68% chance that the true percentage in the population that would answer "yes" is between 57% and 63% (i.e., 60% – 6 = 54% and 60% + 6 = 66%). These values (54% and 66%) are what is known as the *limits of the 68% confidence interval.*

If the standard error is multiplied by two, we can create a 95% confidence interval. Continuing with the example in the previous paragraph, if we multiply the standard error of 3 by 2, we get 6. Adding and subtracting the 6 from 60%, we can say that odds are 95 out of 100 that the true percentage in the population is between 54% and 66% (i.e., 60% – 6 = 54% and 60% + 6 = 66%). These values (54% and 66%) are what is known as the *limits of the approximate 95% confidence interval.*[1]

Background Note

The researchers drew data from a variety of sources for their journal article. The statistics in Table 1 are from *Child Maltreatment 2001,*[2] a government publication.

Excerpt from the Research Article[3]

Sexually abused children are, as might be predicted, the oldest group. Other age by treatment type interactions are less well known. Children 0 to 2 are more likely than children 6 to 10 or 11 and older to have a most serious abuse type involving neglect (failure to provide) and neglect (failure to supervise). Conversely, children 6 to 10 are more likely than the youngest children to have a most serious abuse type of physical maltreatment.

---

[1] In order to compute the *exact* limits of the 95% confidence interval, multiply the standard error by 1.96 instead of multiplying by 2.

[2] U.S. Department of Health and Human Services Administration for Children and Families (2003). *Child Maltreatment 2001*. Washington, DC: Government Printing Office.

[3] Source: Barth, R. P., Landsverk, J., Chamberlain, P., Reid, J. B., Rolls, J. A., Hurlburt, M. S., Farmer, E. M. Z., James, S., McCabe, K. M., & Kohl, P. L. (2005). Parent-training programs in child welfare services: Planning for a more evidence-based approach to serving biological parents. *Research on Social Work Practice, 15*, 353–371. Copyright © 2005 by Sage Publications. Reprinted with permission.

Table 1
Most Serious Type of Abuse of Children Involved with the Child Welfare System by Age

	Physical maltreatment		Sexual maltreatment		Neglect: Failure to provide		Neglect: Failure to supervise		Other		
	%*	SE	%*	SE	%*	SE	%*	SE	%*	SE	Total
Age											
0 to 2	22.6	2.2	6.1	1.7	29.9	2.5	36.6	3.0	4.8	1.7	100
3 to 5	23.6	2.9	12.8	2.8	23.8	3.8	30.3	2.6	9.5	2.3	100
6 to 10	31.2	2.6	11.1	2.4	18.9	2.4	26.1	2.4	12.7	2.1	100
11+	32.7	3.1	14.9	2.1	12.7	2.3	29.7	2.5	10.0	1.8	100
Total	28.4	1.5	11.5	1.2	20.4	1.5	29.8	1.5	9.9	1.2	100

Source: U.S. DHHS, 2003.
*Percentages may not total to 100 because of rounding.

Questions for Exercise 54

Part A: Factual Questions

1. Which age group had the lowest percentage for "Physical maltreatment"?

2. What percentage of the total sample had "Physical maltreatment"?

3. For the total sample, the percentage for "Neglect: Failure to provide" is 20.4%. What are the limits of the 68% confidence interval for this percentage?

4. For the total sample, the percentage for "Neglect: Failure to provide" is 20.4%. What are the limits of the approximate 95% confidence interval for this percentage?

5. What are the limits of the 68% confidence interval for "Physical maltreatment" for ages 0 to 2?

6. What are the limits of the 68% confidence interval for "Physical maltreatment" for ages 11 and up?

7. Compare your answers to Questions 5 and 6. Do the two confidence intervals overlap (i.e., do any of the percentages in one interval include one or more percentages from the other interval)?

8. What are the limits of the approximate 95% confidence interval for "Physical maltreatment" for ages 11 and up?

9. Compare your answers to Questions 6 and 8. Which confidence interval is larger?

   A. The 68% confidence interval in Question 6
   B. The 95% confidence interval in Question 8

Part B: Questions for Discussion

10. In your opinion, how important is it for researchers to report standard errors when reporting percentages based on a sample from a population? In other words, how much less informative would Table 1 be if all the standard errors had been omitted?

11. Compare your answers to Questions 3 and 4. Note that the 95% confidence interval is larger than the 68% confidence interval. Does this make sense? Explain.

12. Note that in the table all the standard errors for the total sample are smaller than any of the standard errors for any of the age subgroups. Speculate on why this is so.

Exercise 55   Grandparent Roles

Chi-Square: I

Statistical Guide

Chi-square is a test of the significance of the differences among frequencies. Its symbol is χ^2. The null hypothesis for a chi-square test asserts that a difference was created by random sampling error. Like other significance tests, a null hypothesis is rejected when the probability that it is true is low—such as .05, .01, .001, or less. When a null hypothesis is rejected, the difference is declared to be statistically significant. The lower the probability, the more significant the difference. Thus, for instance, the .01 level is more significant than the .05 level.

Note that if the frequencies are significantly different, the percentages based on them are also significantly different. Also, note that in tables that present the results of chi-square tests, it is customary to footnote only those differences that were declared to be statistically significant.

Excerpt from the Research Article[1]

Two independent (unrelated) sample groups of parents and grandparents were recruited.... A total of 105 young adult parents, between the ages of 21 and 40 years, participated in this study.... A total of 105 middle-aged and older grandparents, ranging in age from 36 to 84 years ($M = 64$ years) also participated in this study. This group is defined as grandparents of any age, sex, or race who are (a) not serving as a primary caregiver to their grandchildren; (b) residing in a separate household from their grandchildren; and (c) living within a one-hour drive, or 50 miles, from their grandchildren.

The grandparent participants were more likely than young adult parents to rank the roles of religious guide ($\chi^2 = 34.1$, $p < .001$) and family historian ($\chi^2 = 6.18$, $p < .05$) as important. Also, grandparents were more likely than parents to rank the role of playmate as important to initiate with young grandchildren ($\chi^2 = 23.31$, $p < .001$).

Table 2
Intergenerational Perspectives on the Grandparent Role

Specific grandparent role	% of parents ranking role important	% of grandparents ranking role important
Friend	68	82
Teacher	60	76
Role model	55	66
Companion	45	54
Playmate**	52	76
Family historian*	39	64
Religious guide**	24	56
Mediator	26	31
Chauffeur	26	28

**$p < .001$. * $p < .05$

[1] Source: Dellmann-Jenkins, M., Hollis, A. H., & Gordon, K. L. (2005). An intergenerational perspective on grandparent roles: Views of young parents and middle-age/older adults. *Journal of Intergenerational Relationships, 3*, 35–48. Copyright © 2005 by The Haworth Press, Inc. Reprinted with permission.

Questions for Exercise 55

Part A: Factual Questions

1. What percentage of grandparents thought the role of being "Family historian" was important?

2. The smallest percentage of grandparents regarded which role as important?

3. Based on the information in Table 2, how many null hypotheses should be rejected?

4. Is the difference between parents and grandparents on the importance of the role of a friend statistically significant? If yes, at what probability level?

5. Is the difference between parents and grandparents on the importance of the role of a "Playmate" statistically significant? If yes, at what probability level?

6. Should the null hypothesis for the difference between parents and grandparents on the importance of the role of a "Teacher" be rejected? Explain.

7. The difference between parents and grandparents is more highly significant for which one of the following roles?

    A. Friend   B. Family historian   C. Religious guide

8. The difference between parents and grandparents is more highly significant for which one of the following roles?

    A. Playmate   B. Family historian   C. Role model

Part B: Questions for Discussion

9. Do any of the differences between parents' and grandparents' perspectives, as indicated in Table 2, surprise you? Why? Why not?

10. What is your opinion on the researchers' decision to restrict the study to grandparents who were (a) not serving as a primary caregiver to their grandchildren; (b) residing in a separate household from their grandchildren; and (c) living within a one-hour drive, or 50 miles, from their grandchildren?

11. Table 2 contains percentages but not the frequencies. For instance, 60% of the 105 parents thought that the role of "Teacher" was important. By multiplying 0.60 times 105, the consumer of the research can determine that 63 of the parents thought that the role of "Teacher" was important. In your opinion, should the researchers have included such frequencies along with the percentages in the table?

Exercise 56 Money Management

Chi-Square: II

Statistical Guide

To review how to calculate underlying frequencies based on percentages, see the statistical guide for Exercise 1. To review chi-square, see the statistical guide for Exercise 55.

Background Notes

Although it is traditional to report values of chi-square with the associated probabilities, some researchers report only the probabilities, as in the excerpt below. Because decisions are based on the probability levels, the results of the chi-square test can be interpreted without the chi-square values.

Excerpt from the Research Article[1]

Thirty-five people were recruited through ABD (acquired brain dysfunction) case management and accommodation services [primarily those with alcohol-related brain injury].

In addition, 15 healthy community volunteers were recruited through advertisements.... This control group was matched with the clinical sample on a number of relevant demographic variables, including age, gender, and main source of income.... The control group was also matched as closely as possible to the clinical sample on years of education and National Adult Reading Test....

Table 1

Percentage of Participants with Money Management Problems in the ABD and Control Groups

Money management problem	ABD ($n = 32$)	Control ($n = 15$)	p
Problems with ATM	37	0	.001
Don't often check change	42	18	.064
Pay bills or rent late	66	47	.219
Thrown out of accommodation	3.2	0	.371
Owe money for debts	22	6.7	.166
Spend all money within first few days	59	20	.010
Go without essentials	25	0	.009
Very problematic impulse buying	56	6.7	.000
Spend all money on things they like	47	6.7	.003
Need to borrow money	52	20	.036

Note. ABD = acquired brain dysfunction; ATM = automatic teller machine.

---

[1] Source: Hoskin, K. M., Jackson, M., & Crowe, S. F. (2005). Money management after acquired brain dysfunction: The validity of neuropsychological assessment. *Rehabilitation Psychology, 50,* 355–365. Copyright © 2005 by the Educational Publishing Foundation. Reprinted with permission.

Questions for Exercise 56

Part A: Factual Questions

1. What percentage of the control group "Pay bills or rent late"?

2. The table shows that 20% of the 15 members of the control group "Need to borrow money." How many of the 15 need to borrow money?

3. The table shows that 56% of the 32 members of the ABD group have "Very problematic impulse buying." How many of the 32 have this problem?

4. Using conventional standards, should the null hypothesis be rejected for the problem of "Don't often check change"? Explain your reasoning.

5. Using conventional standards, should the null hypothesis be rejected for the problem of "Need to borrow money"? Explain your reasoning.

6. Using conventional standards, should the difference for "Go without essentials" be rejected at the .001 level? Explain your reasoning.

7. Using conventional standards, should the difference for "Need to borrow money" be rejected at the .05 level? Explain your reasoning.

8. The differences for "Problems with ATM" and "Spend all money within first few days" are both statistically significant. Which one is more significant?

9. Using .05 as the minimum level for significance, how many of the 10 differences in the table are statistically significant?

Part B: Question for Discussion

10. The control group was matched with the ABD sample on demographic characteristics. In your opinion, is matching an important element in this study? Explain.

Exercise 57   Self-Employed Hispanic Persons by Gender

Chi-Square: III

Statistical Guide

To review chi-square, see the statistical guide for Exercise 55. Note that in the excerpt below, the .10 probability level is reported in addition to the more traditional .05 and .01 levels. Also, note that chi-square values are given only for comparisons that are statistically significant.

The statistics in the excerpt are for Hispanics residing in California. The data were originally collected by the United States Census Bureau, which used a sample of California residents.

Excerpt from the Research Article[1]

The sampling frame included the following: only heads of households, persons 16 years of age and older who self-identified as Hispanic regardless of race, householders who worked at some point [during the year], and householders who were employed in their own unincorporated business and professional practice.... The final sample consisted of 7,760 Hispanic self-employed persons, 64% (n = 4,931) who were self-employed men and 36% (n = 2,829) who were self-employed women.

Table 1
Percentages of Variables for Self-Employed Hispanic Persons by Gender

Variable	Self-employed men	Self-employed women	Test statistic for difference between samples
Occupation			
Managerial and professional	19.0%	14.7%	$\chi^2 = 22.27$***
Technical, sales, or administrative	16.9%	20.9%	$\chi^2 = 18.77$***
Service	8.9%	55.1%	$\chi^2 = 2012.26$***
Farm, forestry, and fishing	14.8%	1.4%	$\chi^2 = 359.65$***
Craft, precision production, and repair	29.4%	3.1%	$\chi^2 = 785.47$***
Operators, fabricators, and laborers	11.0%	4.7%	$\chi^2 = 87.99$***
Education			
Less than high school	48.7%	48.3%	
High school graduate	18.9%	20.5%	$\chi^2 = 3.07$*
Some college	22.1%	22.5%	
Bachelor's degree or more	10.4%	8.7%	$\chi^2 = 5.81$**
Immigrated to the United States	62.2%	62.5%	

* $p < .10$, ** $p < .05$, *** $p < .01$.

---

[1] Source: Zuiker, V. S., Katras, M. J., Montalto, C. P., & Olson, P. D. (2003). Hispanic self-employment: Does gender matter? *Hispanic Journal of Behavioral Sciences, 25,* 73–94. Copyright © 2003 by Sage Publications. Reprinted with permission.

Questions for Exercise 57

Part A: Factual Questions

1. How many more men than women in the sample were self-employed?

2. For which occupation is there the largest difference between men and women?

3. What is the value of chi-square for the occupation of "Operators, fabricators, and laborers"?

4. What is the value of p for the difference between the percentage of men who are "Operators, fabricators, and laborers" and the percentage of women who are "Operators, fabricators, and laborers"?

5. Based on your answer to Question 4, should the difference be declared to be statistically significant?

6. Are all the differences between occupations statistically significant at the same probability level? If yes, at what level?

7. Compare the probability level for "High school graduate" with the probability level for "Bachelor's degree or more." Which one is more significant? Explain.

8. Should the null hypothesis be rejected for the difference in the percentages of men and women for "Craft, precision production, and repair"? Why? Why not?

9. Is the difference for "Some college" statistically significant? Explain the basis for your answer.

10. Should the null hypothesis for "Immigrated to the United States" be rejected? Explain the basis for your answer.

Part B: Questions for Discussion

11. If you have a statistics textbook, determine if the textbook author discusses the use of the $p < .10$ level in significance testing. Write your findings here.

12. Are the differences in occupations surprising to you? Explain.

13. In your opinion, are the differences between men and women in occupations or in amount of education more dramatic? Explain.

Exercise 58   Gender Differences in Drinking Problems

Chi-Square and Cramer's V

Statistical Guide

To review chi-square, see the statistical guide for Exercise 55. In the following excerpt, chi-square was used to determine the significance of the differences between females and males.

Cramer's V is a measure of association used for nominal data. For all practical purposes, it can be interpreted like a Pearson r correlation coefficient (see the statistical guideline for Exercise 25). Note that while the interpretation is similar, the Pearson r is used to describe the association between two sets of scores (at the ordinal or interval level of measurement), while Cramer's V describes the strength of association or dependency between two nominal (i.e., categorical) variables.

Note that f is the symbol for "frequency."

Excerpt from the Research Article[1]

College freshmen (age $M = 18.24$)...responded to an anonymous questionnaire...as part of an adjudication process for having been cited by campus authorities...for violating rules concerning under-aged drinking or the use of illicit drugs.

The Alcohol Change Index (ACI)...is a single-item question: "In the past three months, how would you describe your pattern of alcohol use?" Responses were classified as "increased drinking" or "not increased drinking."

Binge drinking measures whether or not participants consumed five or more drinks at one sitting within the past two weeks (four or more for women).

Heavy drinking was indicated by usually drinking five or more drinks per week.

The ten-question AUDIT includes three questions on alcohol consumption, four questions on dependence, and three on consequences. A respondent who obtains a cut-off score of greater than or equal to eight is considered a problem drinker in this analysis.

The College Alcohol Problem Scale asks "How often have you had any of the following problems over the past year as a result of drinking too much alcohol?" Because the subscale for distributions are very positively skewed, both the personal and social problem subscales were recoded into dichotomous measures (experienced one or more incidents of a problem or did not)....

Table 1

Univariate Data for Major Factors for Total Sample (n = 389) and by Women (n = 143) and Men (246)

	Total		Female		Male			
	f	%	f	%	f	%	Chi-square	Cramer's V
ACI	73	18.8	23	16.1	50	20.3	.99	
Binge drinking	241	62.0	66	46.2	175	71.1	23.98**	.25**
Heavy drinking	142	36.5	31	21.7	111	45.1	21.44**	.24**
AUDIT (≥ 8)	257	66.1	73	51.0	184	74.8	22.75**	.24**
Personal problems	145	37.3	47	32.9	98	39.8	1.88	
Social problems	191	49.1	55	38.5	136	55.3	10.24**	.16**

$**p < .01$

---

[1] Source: O'Hare, T. (2005). Comparing the AUDIT and 3 drinking indices as predictors of personal and social drinking problems in freshman first offenders. *Journal of Alcohol and Drug Education, 49*, 37–61. Copyright © 2005 by the American Alcohol and Drug Information Foundation. Reprinted with permission.

Questions for Exercise 58

Part A: Factual Questions

1. What percentage of the females reported "Binge drinking"?

2. What percentage of the males reported "Binge drinking"?

3. Was the null hypothesis rejected for the difference on "Binge drinking"? If yes, at what probability level?

4. Was the difference for the difference on "Binge drinking" statistically significant? If yes, at what probability level?

5. Consider the value of Cramer's V for "Binge drinking." Does Cramer's V indicate that there is a very strong relationship? Explain.

6. Four of the chi-square tests are statistically significant. For which one is the relationship the weakest? (Hint: Examine the values of Cramer's V.) Explain.

7. Four of the chi-square tests are statistically significant. For which one is the relationship the strongest? Explain.

8. For which two variables should the null hypothesis not be rejected?

Part B: Questions for Discussion

9. Notice that the researcher reported values of Cramer's V for only four of the six variables. Speculate on why he did not report the values for all six.

10. All the percentages for females are lower than the corresponding percentages for males. Does this surprise you? Explain.

Exercise 59 Personality Disorders and Substance Use

Chi-Square and Odds Ratio

Statistical Guide

To review the chi-square test, including how to interpret probabilities (i.e., p values), see the statistical guide for Exercise 55.

When an *odds ratio* (*OR*) equals 1.00, it means that the odds that something will happen to one group are equal to the odds that it will happen to another group. For instance, if we compare the lung cancer rates for one group that regularly drinks tap water with another group that regularly drinks bottled water, we might expect to get an odds ratio of about 1.00, indicating that the odds that the members of the two groups would get lung cancer are equal. On the other hand, if we compared lung cancer rates for groups that smoke and do not smoke, we would expect a much higher odds ratio. For the sake of argument, let us say that the odds ratio in one study of this issue is 3.50. For all practical purposes, we can interpret this as indicating that the odds of getting lung cancer if an individual smokes are 3.50 times greater than the odds of getting lung cancer if an individual does not smoke.

Because of random errors, an odds ratio will sometimes be greater than 1.00 even if there is no true difference. For instance, in a study of the effects of tap versus bottled water on lung cancer rates, another researcher might get an *OR* of 1.32. Whether this is meaningful or not can be determined by examining the associated test of statistical significance such as the chi-square test. If chi-square indicates that the comparison is not statistically significant, the *OR* of 1.32 can be interpreted as not being significantly greater than 1.00.

Excerpt from the Research Article[1]

The participants were 121 adolescents who met inclusion (ages 15 to 18 and English-speaking) and exclusion (mental retardation, organic mental disorder, or had less than nine years of education) criteria and provided both their own and their parents' informed consent. There were 84 females (69%) and 37 males (31%). The mean age of the sample was 16.3 years...; 70.2% were Caucasian, 3.3% African American, 22.3% Hispanic or Latino, 1.7% Asian, and 2.5% other.

Of the 121 participants, 38 (31%) were diagnosed with one or more personality disorders. Eleven (30%) of the 37 males and 27 (32%) of the 84 females were diagnosed with personality disorders (chi-square = 0.07, $p > .05$).

Analyses of distributions of substance use among individuals meeting and not meeting diagnostic criteria for personality disorders (PD) were conducted to determine whether those diagnosed with personality disorders would report more frequent substance use than those not so diagnosed. (See Table 1 on the next page.)

---

[1] Source: Serman, N., Johnson, J. G., Geller, P. A., Kanost, R. E., & Zacharapoulou, H. (2002). Personality disorders associated with substance use among American and Greek adolescents. *Adolescence, 37,* 841–854. Copyright © 2002 by Libra Publishers, Inc. Reprinted with permission.

Table 1

Substance Use Among Adolescents with and without Personality Disorders

Substance use	PD absent		PD present		χ^2	Odds Ratio
	n	%	*n*	%		
Cigarette smoking						
Past year					0.07	1.11
No use in past year	48	58%	21	55%		
Some use in past year	35	42%	17	45%		
Past 30 days (daily use)					0.07	1.13
≤ 1 cigarette per day	63	76%	28	74%		
> 1 cigarette per day	20	24%	10	26%		
Alcohol consumption						
Past year					7.85**	5.32
No use in past year	26	31%	3	8%		
Some use in past year	57	69%	35	92%		
Past 30 days (≥ 5 drinks per day)					4.26*	2.91
0–1 occasions	75	90%	29	76%		
> 1 occasion	8	10%	9	24%		

Note. PD absent, $n = 83$; PD present, $n = 38$.
*$p < .05$, **$p < .01$.

Questions for Exercise 59

Part A: Factual Questions

1. Thirty percent of the males were diagnosed with one or more personality disorders, while 32 percent of the females had this diagnosis. Is the difference between these two percentages statistically significant? Explain the basis for your answer.

2. What percentage of those with personality disorders consumed some alcohol in the past year?

3. What percentage of those without personality disorders consumed some alcohol in the past year?

4. The researchers conducted a chi-square test to examine whether those with personality disorders and those without them differed significantly in terms of alcohol consumption in the past year. What was the value of this chi-square?

5. Is the value of chi-square for Question 4 statistically significant? If so, at what probability level was it significant?

6. The researchers conducted a chi-square test to examine whether those with personality disorders and those without them differed significantly in terms of cigarette smoking in the past year. What was the value of this chi-square?

7. Is the value of chi-square for Question 6 statistically significant? If so, at what probability level was it significant?

8. Which of the following is statistically significant at a higher level (i.e., more statistically significant)? Explain the basis for your answer.

   A. Differences for alcohol consumption in the past year
   B. Differences for alcohol consumption in the past 30 days

9. What is the odds ratio (*OR*) for daily cigarette smoking for the past 30 days for those who have personality disorders compared with those who do not have these disorders?

10. Having personality disorders puts individuals at greatest risk for which one of these behaviors? Explain the basis for your answer.

    A. Cigarette smoking in the past year
    B. Alcohol consumption in the past 30 days

11. The *OR* associated with personality disorders for alcohol consumption in the past year is 5.32. Is this significantly greater than an *OR* of 1.00? Explain the basis for your answer.

Part B: Questions for Discussion

12. Do you think it was a good idea to exclude potential participants who had less than nine years of education? Explain.

13. The racial/ethnic composition of the sample is different from the composition of the general population. For instance, African Americans are underrepresented. In your opinion, is this important? Explain.

14. In this study, all adolescents with personality disorders were put into one group for the analysis. Do you think that in a future study it would be productive to study separately the effects of various types of disorders (e.g., passive–aggressive personalities, overly dependent personalities, and antisocial personalities) on substance use? Explain.

Exercise 60   Duration of Homelessness

Standard Error of the Median and 68% and 95% Confidence Intervals

Statistical Guide

To review the meaning of the median, see the statistical guide for Exercise 11. To review the concepts of standard error and 95% confidence interval (CI), see the statistical guide for Exercise 35. While the guide for Exercise 35 deals with how these statistics apply to means, the guidelines for that exercise also apply to the interpretation of standard errors for medians and the associated confidence intervals. As you may recall from Exercise 36, for a 68% confidence interval, add the standard error of the mean to determine the upper limit, and then subtract the standard error of the mean to determine the lower limit. The same procedure applies to medians.

Excerpt from the Research Article[1]

We recruited 445 men and women who were homeless and without kin from the municipal shelter care system for homeless adults in New York City.

[After voluntary informed consent was obtained], participants were carefully tracked throughout the 18-month follow-up period to document the number of days spent [homeless].

Table 1
Duration of Homelessness During the 18-Month Follow-Up Period

	Sample %	No. of days homeless, median	SE	95% CI
Age, y.				
18–29	31	168	17	134, 202
30–44	39	182	26	131, 233
> 44	30	269	47	178, 360
Gender				
Male	48	188	21	146, 230
Female	52	194	22	151, 237
Race/ethnicity				
White/other	35	182	29	126, 238
Black	65	194	19	156, 232
Citizenship				
American born	85	196	17	163, 229
Foreign born–U.S. citizen	5	147	68	13, 281
Foreign born–foreign citizen	9	189	53	85, 293
Veteran status				
Nonveteran	90	185	11	162, 208
Veteran	10	326	77	175, 477
Education				
≤ High school	66	189	21	149, 229
> High school	34	196	18	160, 232
Marital status				
Single (never married)	60	188	12	165, 211
Other	40	196	39	119, 273
Past employment status				
Employed	56	175	16	144, 206
Unemployed	44	247	32	184, 310
Current employment status				
Employed	12	126	33	61, 191
Unemployed	88	201	18	166, 236

---

[1] Source: Caton, C. L. M., Dominguez, B., Schanzer, B., Hasin, D. S., Shrout, P. E., Felix, A., McQuistion, H., Opler, L. A., & Hsu, E. (2005). Risk factors for long-term homelessness: Findings from a longitudinal study of first-time homeless single adults. *American Journal of Public Health, 95,* 1753–1759. Copyright © 2005 by the American Public Health Association. Reprinted with permission.

Questions for Exercise 60

Part A: Factual Questions

1. On the average, did younger *or* older participants remain homeless a larger number of days? Explain.

2. What percentage of the males spent less than 188 days homeless? Explain the basis for your answer.

3. What percentage of the males spent more than 188 days homeless? Explain the basis for your answer.

4. What are the limits of the 68% CI for females on the number of days homeless?

5. What are the limits of the 95% CI for females on the number of days homeless?

6. What is the median for number of days homeless for veterans?

7. What are the limits of the 68% CI for those with more than a high school education?

8. What are the limits of the 95% CI for those with more than a high school education?

Part B: Questions for Discussion

9. Compare your answers to Questions 4 and 5. If your answers are correct, the 95% confidence interval is larger than the 68% confidence interval. Does this make sense? Explain.

10. In your opinion, do the statistics suggest that past employment status is predictive of the duration of homelessness?

11. In their research article, the researchers refer to their study as a "preliminary study." In your opinion, what aspects of the study, if any, qualify it as preliminary?

12. Are the results of this study interesting or surprising to you? Explain.

Exercise 61   Fathers' Values for Their Newborns

Wilcoxon-Mann-Whitney Test

Statistical Guide

To review the meaning of the *median*, see the statistical guide for Exercise 11. Note that the median is appropriate for averaging ranks.

The *Wilcoxon-Mann-Whitney test* (also known as *the Mann-Whitney U test* or the *Wilcoxon rank sum test*) is a test of statistical significance for use with two independent groups. Unlike the *t* test or ANOVA, this test is appropriate when the data are in the form of ranks (i.e., ordinal data).

Like other significance tests, when the Mann-Whitney *U* test indicates that *p* is equal to or less than .05, researchers declare the difference to be statistically significant (i.e., they reject the null hypothesis). The smaller the value of *p*, the more significant the difference.

In the excerpt, the researchers use the term "alpha level," which refers to the probability level at which they were willing to declare significance.

In a table showing significant differences, the absence of a probability value for a comparison indicates that the difference is not statistically significant.

Background Notes

The fathers ranked the 18 values in Table 3, giving a rank of 1 to the value that they most wanted for their newborns, a rank of 2 for the value they next most wanted, and so on. For each value, the median (*Mdn*) indicates the average rank given to the value. The ranks in the table are rankings of the medians shown in the table.

Excerpt from the Research Article[1]

Men in the waiting room of a maternity ward in a large public hospital, which serves primarily the inner city, and men in the waiting room of a maternity ward in a nearby private hospital, which serves primarily the middle class, participated....

Inner-city fathers were younger, less educated, and less likely to be employed than the middle-class fathers. Inner-city fathers were more likely to be Hispanic and Catholic.

The Wilcoxon-Mann-Whitney test with an alpha level of .05 was used for value comparisons...of fathers.

Inner-city fathers emphasized instrumental values connected to conformity and self-control in children while middle-class fathers emphasized personal qualities involving resources of the mind, such as "imaginative" and "intellectual." Middle-class fathers also emphasized values connected to benevolence, such as "loving" and "honest."

---

[1] Source: Minton, J., Shell, J., & Solomon, L. Z. (2005). Values of fathers for themselves and their newborns. *Psychological Reports, 96,* 323–333. Copyright © 2005 by Psychological Reports. Reprinted with permission.

Table 3

Rokeach Instrumental Scale: Median Ranks and Rank Order of Fathers' Instrumental Values for Child

| | Rank | | | | |
| | Inner-city fathers ($n = 95$) | | Middle-class fathers ($n = 28$) | | |
Value	*Mdn*	Rank order	*Mdn*	Rank order	Wilcoxon-Mann-Whitney Z
Ambitious	6.50	2	8.00	6	.72
Broadminded	10.30	13	9.25	10	.50
Capable	8.70	5	11.50	13	2.00‡
Cheerful	10.75	14	7.42	5	.88
Clean	10.77	15	16.67	18	4.20*
Courageous	9.17	6	8.40	8	.07
Forgiving	10.00	12	9.50	11	.13
Helpful	10.81	16	11.33	12	.87
Honest	6.21	1	2.50	1	3.04†
Imaginative	13.93	18	8.50	9	3.60*
Independent	9.94	11	8.33	7	1.68
Intellectual	9.79	9	7.25	4	2.02‡
Logical	13.61	17	14.20	16	.61
Loving	7.00	4	3.25	2	3.81*
Obedient	9.88	10	15.20	17	3.31*
Polite	9.75	8	12.25	15	1.99‡
Responsible	6.80	3	6.50	3	.49
Self-controlled	9.28	7	12.20	14	2.27‡

*$p < .001$. †$p < .01$. ‡$p < .05$.

Questions for Exercise 61

Part A: Factual Questions

1. What is the median rank for "Loving" for the inner-city fathers?

2. What percentage of the inner-city fathers gave "Loving" a rank of more than 7?

3. Which value was most highly desired by the inner-city fathers? (Hint: A lower rank indicates a greater desire because a rank of 1 is given to the most desired value.)

4. According to the medians, which group had a greater desire for "Intellectual"? (Hint: A rank of 1 indicates the greatest desire; a rank of 2 indicates less desire than a rank of 1.)

5. Was the difference referred to in Question 4 statistically significant at the .05 level?

6. Should the null hypothesis for the difference in Question 4 be rejected at the .05 level?

7. According to the medians, which group had a greater desire for "Obedient"?

8. Was the difference referred to in Question 7 statistically significant? If yes, at what probability level?

9. Should the null hypothesis for the difference in Question 7 be rejected? If yes, at what probability level?

10. The difference between the two groups of fathers was statistically significant at a higher level for the value of being (explain your choice)

    A. "Polite."
    B. "Obedient."

11. The difference between the two groups of fathers was statistically significant at a higher level for the value of being (explain your choice)

    A. "Capable."
    B. "Clean."

Part B: Questions for Discussion

12. The researchers state that "…middle-class fathers emphasized personal qualities involving resources of the mind, such as 'imaginative'…." Do the values in the table support this statement? Explain.

13. In addition to differing in terms of being inner-city versus middle-class, the two groups of fathers also differed in their religion and ethnicity. In your opinion, is it important to consider these additional differences when interpreting the results of this study? Explain.

14. Are the results of this study interesting or surprising to you? Explain.

Exercise 62   Effectiveness of an AIDS Prevention Program

Wilcoxon Matched-Pairs Test

Statistical Guide

The Wilcoxon matched-pairs test determines the significance of the difference between two sets of ranks obtained from matched pairs. For example, a person's rank on a pretest (before treatment) may be matched with the same person's rank on a posttest (after treatment).

Like other significance tests, when the Wilcoxon matched-pairs test indicates that p is equal to or less than .05, we usually declare the difference to be statistically significant (i.e., reject the null hypothesis). The smaller the value of p, the more significant the difference.

Excerpt from the Research Article[1]

SECRETS, an AIDS prevention program, was a theatrical production performed by young actors portraying adolescents.... SECRETS provided HIV/AIDS information and role-modeled HIV risk-reduction behaviors.

Data on sexual risk-taking behavior were collected prior to and three months after students attended the AIDS prevention program. Sexual risk-taking behavior was considered one variable by summing the frequency of six behaviors [such as number of times a student engaged in sexual intercourse without using a condom and number of sexual partners]. The responses were from 0 to 5 for each behavior with a potential range from 0 to 30.

The sample, at pretest, had a relatively low level of sexual risk-taking behavior. The mean sexual risk-taking score was 1.8 ($SD = 3.5$).... The sexual risk-taking scores ranged from 0 to 19 for this sample.

As the majority had not had sexual intercourse and there was a great variance in sexual behavior, the sample was categorized as low (≤ 1.8) and high (> 1.8) sexual risk-taking groups.... The Wilcoxon matched-pairs test was performed for the low- and high-risk sexual risk-taking groups.

There was a significant difference between the pre- and posttest sexual risk-taking behavior for the low-risk group, Wilcoxon (129) = –4.9, $p = .0000$. For the low-risk group, 100 out of 127 (79%) had lower scores at posttest than at pretest.

There was also a significant difference between pre- and posttest sexual risk-taking behavior for the high-risk group, Wilcoxon (52) = –2.1, $p = .04$. For the high-risk group, 32 out of 52 (62%) had lower scores at posttest than at pretest.

The findings of the study suggested support for SECRETS in decreasing sexual risk-taking behavior among high school students.

---

[1] Source: Hanna, K. M., Hanrahan, S., Hershey, J., & Greer, D. (1997). Evaluation of the effect of an AIDS prevention program on high school students' sexual risk-taking behavior. *Issues in Comprehensive Pediatric Nursing, 20*, 25–34. Copyright © Taylor and Francis, 1997. Reprinted with permission.

Questions for Exercise 62

Part A: Factual Questions

1. For all students, what was the average pretest score?

2. Is the distribution for all students on the pretest skewed? If yes, is it a positive *or* negative skew? (Hint: Consider the mean and the range.)

3. The researchers state that "there was a great variance in sexual behavior." What specific statistics were reported that give more information on this matter?

4. A student with a score on the pretest of 2 would have been classified as belonging to which group?

5. For the low-risk group, should the null hypothesis be rejected? Explain.

6. For the high-risk group, should the null hypothesis be rejected? Explain.

7. For which of the tests was the level of significance higher? Explain the basis for your choice.
   A. The one for the high-risk group
   B. The one for the low-risk group

8. Was the test for the low-risk group statistically significant at the .001 level? Explain.

9. Was the difference for the high-risk group statistically significant at the .05 level? Explain.

Part B: Questions for Discussion

10. The researchers reported the average pretest score for all students but not the corresponding post-test score. Speculate on why they did not report the latter.

11. Was there a control group in this study? Explain.

12. In their article, the researchers mention that the sample included only students who had consented to be in the study and also had parental consent for them to participate. Consent was provided by 36% of parents and participants. Is this a limitation of the study? Explain.

13. Speculate on why the researchers used the Wilcoxon matched-pairs test instead of a *t* test or ANOVA.